A GUIDE FOR MEN TO BREAK THROUGH

MASTERING

ANY SETBACK TO REACH THEIR FULL POTENTIAL

MENTAL

IN LIFE AND SPORTS

STRENGTH

JAMES CARD

Contents

About the Author 7
Introduction 8
    About This Book 11
Chapter 1: What is Mental Strength? 13
    More Than Just Toughness 16
    Components of Mental Strength 17
    Nature vs. Nurture Debate on Mental Strength 19
        Nature: The Innate Traits 19
        Nurture: The Development of Traits 19
        Finding the Balance 20
    Reflection Questions 21
    Summing Up 21
Chapter 2: The Evolution of Male Mental Toughness 23
    Lessons from History 25
        The Myth of the Stoic Warrior 26
        Modern Understanding of Mental Strength 28
    The Power Within 29
        Mental Strength: A Learnable Skill 29
        Understanding Self-Doubt and Anxiety 30
    Why Willpower and Motivation Are Not Enough 31
    Reflection Questions 32
    Summing Up 32
Chapter 3: Mental Strength as the Answer 35
    The Crucial Role of Mental Strength 38
    Learning from Legends 39
        Serena Williams: Embracing Challenges and Bouncing Back 39
        Muhammad Ali: Courage and Conviction 40
        Tom Brady: The Power of Persistence 41
        David Beckham: Grace Under Pressure 41
        Pelé: Passion and Resilience 42
    The Problem with "Push Through the Pain" 42
    Shifting Mindsets and Reprogramming Thought Patterns 43
        Embracing Setbacks as Opportunities 43
    Reflection Questions 44
    Summing Up 44

Chapter 4: Self-Awareness and Growth Mindset 47
- The Power of Self-Awareness 51
- The Growth Mindset: A Game-Changer 52
  - Fixed vs. Growth Mindsets 52
- Cultivating a Growth Mindset 55
- The Role of Self-Compassion 56
- Turning Insights into Action 57
- Reflection Questions 59
- Summing Up 59

Chapter 5: What's Really Holding You Back? 61
- The Fear Factor 63
- A Comparison Trap 64
- The Comfort Zone Conundrum 65
- Becoming Your Own Cheerleader 65
  - What Are Positive and Negative Affirmations? 66
- Staying Present and Focused With Mindfulness 67
- Reflection Questions 69
- Summing Up 69

Chapter 6: Unlocking Peak Performance 71
- The Top Seven Traits of Mentally Strong People 74
  - 1. Facing Reality and Challenges Directly 75
  - 2. Accepting Responsibility for Choices 75
  - 3. Self-Monitoring and Self-Correcting 75
  - 4. Finding Meaning in Past Experiences 75
  - 5. Balancing Emotions and Facts 76
  - 6. Addressing Past Traumas 76
  - 7. Demonstrating Emotional Intelligence 76
- The Mind's Gymnasium 77
  - Sculpting Mental Muscles with Visualization 77
  - The Self-Talk Symphony 79
  - The Focus Funnel 80
- Reflection Questions 81
- Summing Up 81

Chapter 7: The Mental Rehearsal Method 83
- The Power of Mental Rehearsal 85
- The Neuroscience of Imagination 85
- Conquering Anxiety Through Imagination 86
- From Imagination to Reality 86
  - Practical Steps to Mastering Mental Rehearsal 87

Reflection Questions ... 87
Summing Up ... 88

Chapter 8: The Resilience Playbook: Winning Strategies from Sports and Business ... 89
    Embracing the Unknown ... 91
    5 Daily Habits ... 92
        1. Mindful Meditation ... 92
        2. Self-Care ... 92
        3. Physical Exercise ... 92
        4. Social Connection ... 93
        5. Gratitude Practice ... 93
    Strategies from the World's Best ... 93
        Mindful Meditation: Kobe Bryant ... 94
        Self-Care: Roger Federer ... 94
        Physical Exercise: Michael Phelps ... 94
        Social Connection: Serena Williams ... 95
        Gratitude Practice: Tom Brady ... 95
    Reflection Questions ... 96
    Summing Up ... 96

Chapter 9: 11 Daily Exercises for Peak Performance ... 99
    1. Practice Mindfulness ... 102
    2. Embrace Self-Compassion ... 103
    3. Step Out of Your Comfort Zone ... 103
    4. Acknowledge and Process Your Feelings ... 104
        Example Emotion Log ... 105
    5. Keep a Balanced Perspective ... 105
        Example "3 Ps" ... 106
    6. Practice Self-Care: Fueling Your Mental Engine ... 106
    7. Build Meaningful Connections: The Power of Social Support ... 107
    8. Set Clear Goals and Pursue Them Persistently: The Roadmap to Success ... 107
        Example S.M.A.R.T Goals ... 108
    9. Develop Gratitude: Shifting Your Focus ... 108
    10. Enhance Mental Stamina: Training Your Brain Like a Muscle ... 109
        Example Pomodoro Technique ... 110
    11. Engage in Brain-Boosting Activities: Cognitive Cross-Training ... 110
    Reflection Questions ... 111
    Summing Up ... 112

Chapter 10: Fireside Reflection ... 113

An Ancient Man's Reflective Practice 117
    Connection to Ancient Wisdom 117
    The Science Behind Reflection 118
    Modern Adaptation 119
How to Practice Fireside Reflection and the Benefits 120
    Relaxation and Contemplation 120
    Creative Thinking and Inspiration 121
    Mindfulness and Stress Reduction: 121
    Candle Meditation and Cognitive Enhancement: 122
    How to Practice Candle Meditation 123
Reflection Questions 124
Summing Up 125
Conclusion 127
References 130

© Copyright 2024 - All rights reserved.

The content of this book may not be reproduced, duplicated, or transmitted without direct written permission from the author or the publisher.

Under no circumstances will any blame or legal responsibility be held against the publisher or author for any damages, reparation, or monetary loss due to the information contained within this book. Either directly or indirectly. You are responsible for your own choices, actions, and results.

Legal Notice:

This book is copyright-protected and only for personal use. You cannot amend, distribute, sell, use, quote, or paraphrase any part of this book's content without the author's or publisher's consent.

Disclaimer Notice:

Please note that the information in this document is for educational and entertainment purposes only. All efforts have been made to present accurate, up-to-date, reliable, and complete information. No warranties of any kind are declared or implied. Readers acknowledge that the author does not render legal, financial, medical, or professional advice. The content within this book has been derived from various sources. The author has no responsibility for the persistence or accuracy of URLs for external or third-party internet websites referred to in this publication and does not guarantee that any content on such websites is, or will remain, accurate or appropriate. Please consult a licensed professional before attempting any techniques outlined in this book.

By reading this document, the reader agrees that the author is under no circumstances responsible for any direct or indirect losses incurred from using the information contained within this document, including, but not limited to, errors, omissions, or inaccuracies.

About the Author

James Card has over two decades of experience as an educator and coach and is a father of boys. His practical, science-backed practical advice on mental strength and building self-awareness, combined with personal experiences empowers individuals to master their minds and conquer life's challenges. Committed to making complex psychological topics accessible to everyone, James guides people on their journey toward mental strength so they can reach their full potential in life and sports.

His book reflects his in-depth research and understanding of mental strength, providing valuable guidance for men seeking to break free from limiting beliefs and patterns of self-sabotage and achieve their full potential.

James' work as an educator has seen countless individuals overcome challenges and achieve their goals. His passion for helping people grow stronger mentally is evident in his career and writing, making his books a valuable resource for anyone looking to improve their life. James instils in readers the desire to practice daily actions that will cultivate the mental strength needed to overcome obstacles and reach their full potential!

Beyond his passion for mental strength training, James nurtures a passion for rugby, camping, hiking, and card nights with mates. When he is not working, you can find him enjoying these pastimes in his Australian home, where he resides with his much-loved family.

Introduction

"My attitude is that if you push me toward something that you think is a weakness, then I will turn that perceived weakness into a strength."
-Michael Jordan

There once was a sophomore in high school who tried out for the varsity basketball team. Unfortunately, he didn't make it. Standing at 5'11" at the time, he was deemed too short to play at that level. It was a tough moment for him.

"Coach, why didn't I make the team?" the teenager asked, feeling heartbroken.

"Well, you've got potential, but you need to work harder," the coach replied.

For many, this setback might have been the end of their basketball dreams. For Jordan, it was just the beginning. Instead of giving up, that teenager used this as motivation. Every day after school, he practiced for hours, determined to prove himself. By his junior year, he made the team and quickly became a standout player.

He made the varsity team the following year and went on to earn a basketball scholarship to the University of North Carolina. From there, his career trajectory is the stuff of legend: six NBA championships, five MVP awards, and a place in basketball history as arguably the greatest player ever (Piccotti, 2023).

Believe it or not, that teenager was Michael Jordan, an iconic figure in the world of basketball and sports in general. It's true, he faced his share of mental challenges throughout his career. His journey to becoming a legend went beyond physical prowess and instead tested his incredible mental strength.

Years later, after joining the Chicago Bulls, Michael faced another big challenge. The Bulls weren't a great team, and they struggled in the playoffs, especially against the tough Detroit Pistons.

"Michael, we need to get stronger," his teammate Scottie Pippen said after another loss to the Pistons.

"I know, Scottie. We'll work harder, get tougher, and we'll beat them," Michael responded.

Michael hit the gym, building his strength and improving his skills. Simultaneously, he focused on mental preparation, developing a relentless mindset that would not allow him to be defeated.

In 1993, tragedy struck when Michael's father was murdered. Deeply affected, Michael decided to retire from basketball and play baseball (Perkins, 2023).

"Are you sure about this, Mike?" his friend asked.

"Yeah, I need a break, and baseball is something my dad and I loved," Michael replied.

This switch to baseball was something that many experts saw as an attempt to cope with grief. Despite the criticism and the struggle of adapting to a new sport, Jordan's time away from basketball was crucial for his mental recovery.

Although many doubted him, Michael pursued baseball

with the same determination he had for basketball. After a year and a half, he realized he missed basketball and decided to return.

"Guess who's back?" Michael said with a smile as he walked into the Bulls' locker room.

When he returned to the NBA in 1995, Jordan was mentally refreshed and more determined than ever. His return wasn't easy, but Michael's mental toughness shone through. He led the Bulls to three consecutive championships from 1996 to 1998, showcasing not just his physical skills but also his unparalleled mental toughness (Piccotti, 2023).

His famous "Flu Game" during the 1997 NBA Finals is a prime example of his mental resilience. Despite being severely ill, Jordan played one of the most iconic games of his career, leading the Bulls to a crucial victory (Williams, 2021).

"Mike, you don't have to play. You're too sick," the team's doctor said.

"No way. My team needs me," Michael insisted, and he went on to score 38 points, leading the Bulls to victory.

This mindset… viewing failures not as endpoints but as stepping stones to success… is at the core of mental strength. Jordan's journey teaches us that mental strength is about perseverance, relentless effort, and the ability to overcome setbacks. His story is a powerful reminder that even the greatest face challenges, but it's how we respond to them that defines our legacy.

…

Now, you might be thinking, "I am nothing like Michael Jordan." But let me ask you this: Have you ever felt insecure, faced grief, or believed you weren't strong enough? Michael Jordan's story shows us that everyone can tap into the same mental strength he did.

Jordan's journey shows us the incredible power of mental resilience. It's not just raw talent or physical gifts that set the greats apart, it's the ability to persevere, push through adversity, and perform at the highest level when it matters most.

About This Book

In this book, we'll explore the secrets to developing unshakeable mental toughness, whether you're an athlete looking to take your game to the next level or simply a man striving to live a more fulfilling life.

Mental strength isn't just about being tough or resilient. It's a combination of emotional intelligence, self-control, resilience, and endurance. And here's the good news—while some may seem naturally mentally tough, these skills can be learned and honed by anyone willing to do the work.

Throughout these pages, you'll discover proven strategies top athletes and high-performers use to manage competitive pressure, overcome self-doubt, and achieve peak performance. From visualization exercises to goal-setting techniques, you'll gain practical tools to conquer your inner critic and unlock your full potential.

But this book isn't just about theory. You'll also receive 11 daily mental strength exercises to help you apply these concepts in your everyday life. These practical exercises will help you build the mental muscle to face any challenge head-on.

Whether you're struggling with self-doubt, battling against adversity, or simply looking to reach new heights in your personal or professional life, this book is your roadmap to mental mastery. It all starts with a commitment to yourself, a willingness to do the work, and a belief in your potential.

As William James, an influential American philosopher and psychologist, once said, "The greatest discovery of my generation is that a human being can alter his life by altering his attitudes." It's time to alter your attitudes, strengthen your mind, and unleash your inner warrior.

Are you ready to master your mental strength and transform your life? Let's begin.

Chapter 1: What is Mental Strength?

*"Always be yourself and have faith in yourself.
Do not go out and look for a successful personality
and try to duplicate it."*
- Bruce Lee

Noah sat on the bench, staring at the basketball court. His team practiced hard, but he couldn't join them that day. He felt overwhelmed by the weight of life's challenges and utterly defeated.

"Hey, Noah, what's going on?" his friend Mike asked, sitting beside him.

Noah sighed, "I just can't do it anymore, Mike. Everything feels too much. Work, family, this team... I don't know how to handle it all."

Mike nodded, understanding. "Life can get pretty overwhelming. But you're not alone in this."

"I feel like I'm always failing," Noah continued. "When something goes wrong, I can't bounce back. I get stuck in this negative loop, doubting myself. My emotions take over, and I lose focus. I keep telling myself I'm not good enough."

Mike put a hand on Noah's shoulder. "We've all been there. It's hard to manage everything, especially when you're under a lot of stress."

Noah shook his head. "I used to be so motivated, but now I just procrastinate. I can't maintain discipline. Fear of failure keeps me from taking risks, and I struggle to adapt when things change. It feels like I'm constantly battling with myself."

Mike looked him in the eye. "You know, everyone deals with setbacks and failures. It's how you respond that matters. You need to work on resilience and managing your emotions better."

Noah sighed again. "I just don't know how. The negative self-talk is relentless. I feel like an imposter, like I don't deserve any of my successes. And I'm burnt out, exhausted from trying to juggle everything."

Mike nodded thoughtfully. "You need to set boundaries. It's okay to say no sometimes and to prioritize your needs. Perfectionism will only hold you back. No one can meet unrealistic standards all the time."

"I guess you're right," Noah said quietly. "But it's hard to change."

There was a moment of silence. But then, Mike remembered something. He had recently read *this* book and transformed his own life based on the techniques he learned. So, he turned to Noah with a smile.

"You know, I've learned some proven strategies and techniques that top athletes and high-performers use to master their mental game. It all starts with developing self-awareness... the ability to understand your thoughts, emotions, and behaviors."

"Seriously?"

"Yeah, man! By gaining insight into your mind, you

can begin to identify the limiting beliefs and negative self-talk that may be holding you back," Mike explained. "But developing mental strength isn't just about changing your mindset—it's also about taking action. It's about daily practice, day in and day out, even when you don't feel like it. It involves daily habits that strengthen your mind and build your resilience."

Noah nodded, absorbing Mike's words. "So, it's more than just being tough?"

"Exactly," Mike said. "Mental strength isn't just about being tough or resilient—it's a combination of emotional intelligence, self-control, resilience, and endurance. And here's the good news: mental strength is not solely determined by genetics. It can be developed through consistent practice and training."

Noah looked thoughtful. "So, anyone can develop mental strength?"

"Absolutely," Mike affirmed. "Developing mental strength is crucial for achieving your full potential in life and sport. It's about pushing through the tough times, maintaining focus and motivation, and bouncing back from setbacks. You can train your mind like your body."

Noah took a deep breath, feeling more hopeful. "Thanks, Mike. I really appreciate this."

"Anytime, Noah," Mike replied with a smile. "Let's get back out there. Remember, it's one step at a time, but each step makes you stronger."

Noah stood up, feeling a renewed sense of determination. With Mike's support and the knowledge that mental strength could be developed, he felt ready to face the court... and life... with a new mindset.

...

Do you feel like Noah? Overwhelmed by life's challenges, struggling to cope with stress, or finding it hard to bounce back from setbacks? Maybe you have trouble managing your emotions, maintaining focus, or dealing with negative self-talk and limiting beliefs. Perhaps procrastination, fear of failure, and imposter syndrome are holding you back. You might even feel burnt out, struggling to set boundaries, or battling perfectionism.

Luckily, this book teaches you all about mental strength. We will show you how to develop the resilience, self-control, and emotional intelligence needed to master your mental game and overcome these obstacles. It's time to build the mental strength necessary to achieve your full potential in life and sport.

More Than Just Toughness

Mental strength is far more than just being tough or resilient. It's a complex and nuanced set of attributes that enable individuals to navigate life's challenges effectively and perform at their best, regardless of circumstances. Mental strength is "the capacity of an individual to deal effectively with stressors, pressures, and challenges and perform to the best of their ability, irrespective of the circumstances in which they find themselves" (Clough 2002). This means it's about building the mental tools to manage stress, adapt to changes, and stay focused on your goals.

This definition shows that mental strength is not about suppressing emotions or putting on a stoic mask. Also, a lot of people think mental strength is something you're either born with, or you're not. But these are misconceptions.

Components of Mental Strength

So, what does mental strength involve? Just like physical strength, mental strength can be developed over time. It takes practice, healthy habits, and a willingness to grow. Let's break it down into its core components to fully understand it.

Type	Definition	Example
Emotional Intelligence	This involves the ability to recognize, understand, and manage your own emotions, as well as the emotions of others. Emotionally intelligent individuals can navigate social situations effectively and maintain healthy relationships, which are crucial for overall mental well-being.	You're on a soccer team, and one of your teammates is upset after missing an important penalty kick. Instead of ignoring them or criticizing their performance, you offer support. *What You Say:* "Hey, I saw how disappointed you are. It's okay to feel that way, but we'll get through this together. Let's focus on our next game and keep improving."
Self-Control	This is the ability to regulate one's thoughts, emotions, and behaviors in the face of temptations and impulses. Self-control is vital for maintaining focus, making rational decisions, and working toward long-term goals.	You're training for a big tennis tournament and are tempted to skip practice to hang out with friends. Instead, you stick to your training schedule. *What You Do:* "I'd love to join my friends, but I've got an important practice session to prepare for the tournament. I'll focus on my drills now and catch up with them later."

Resilience	Often confused with mental strength itself, resilience is actually a component of it. It refers to the ability to bounce back from setbacks, adapt to change, and keep going in the face of adversity.	During your tennis training, you suffer a minor injury. Despite the setback, you continue to attend practice, adapt your training regimen, and stay committed to your goal of competing in the tournament. *What You Do:* "My injury is a setback, but I won't let it derail my training. I'll work with my coach to adjust my practice plan and focus on recovery so I can still perform my best at the tournament."
Endurance	Mental endurance is the capacity to sustain focus, motivation, and effort over extended periods, especially when faced with challenges or monotony.	You're a swimmer preparing for a long-distance event, and your training sessions are becoming repetitive and exhausting. Despite this, you stay focused on your long-term goal. *What You Do:* "These laps are tough and getting monotonous, but I know that pushing through these sessions will get me ready for the competition. I'll keep my eyes on the prize and stay motivated."

These components of mental strength don't just function in isolation. Instead, they weave together to form a solid foundation that helps you tackle life's challenges with grace and determination.

Now, you might be wondering, *Where do these traits come from? Why do some people seem to have them naturally, while I might feel like I'm missing out?*

Nature vs. Nurture Debate on Mental Strength

The debate between nature and nurture asks whether our traits and abilities come from our genetics (nature) or our experiences and environment (nurture). As with many aspects of human psychology, the answer lies somewhere in the middle.

Nature: The Innate Traits

Think of a young athlete with an innate calmness under pressure. This might be due to genetic factors. For instance, research shows that some people are born with a natural ability to manage stress better than others.

While some individuals may have a genetic predisposition toward certain traits contributing to mental strength, this doesn't mean that mental strength is fixed or unchangeable. On the contrary, numerous studies and real-life examples demonstrate that mental strength can be developed and enhanced through deliberate practice and healthy habits.

Nurture: The Development of Traits

On the other hand, nurture refers to how our environment, experiences, and choices shape who we become. This side of the debate argues that our upbringing, education, and life experiences largely influence mental strength.

Consider an athlete who builds resilience through consistent training, overcoming setbacks, and learning from failures. This person might not have been born with an innate talent for handling stress, but through practice and experience, they have developed mental toughness.

As Amy Morin points out, building mental strength involves developing daily habits that build mental muscle and giving up bad habits that hold you back (Morin 2017). This perspective emphasizes the 'nurture' aspect of mental strength, highlighting that regardless of our starting point, we all have the potential to enhance our mental strength through consistent effort and practice.

So, even if you weren't born with certain traits, you can cultivate them over time. Mental strength is not a fixed quality; it can be developed through effort and practice.

Finding the Balance

However, considering all this, research still suggests that genetic and environmental factors significantly shape our mental strength. One study "found that "traits like resilience and self-control… key components of mental strength… are influenced by both genetic predispositions and life experiences" (Plomin et al). While you might see others who appear naturally resilient or emotionally intelligent, this doesn't mean you can't develop these traits yourself. Natural abilities vary, but everyone has a different starting point.

So, mental strength is a vital attribute that goes far beyond mere toughness or resilience. It's a complex interplay of emotional intelligence, self-control, resilience, and endurance that allows individuals to navigate life's challenges effectively and perform at their best. While genetic factors may influence our baseline capacity for mental strength, it is undoubtedly a skill that can be developed and honed over time. By understanding the components of mental strength and committing to its development, individuals can unlock their full potential and thrive in their personal and professional lives.

Reflection Questions

1. Reflect on a recent time when you felt overwhelmed. How did your thoughts and emotions influence your actions? How could increased self-awareness improve your response?
2. Recall a significant setback you faced. How did you handle it? What strategies did you use or could have used to build resilience?
3. Examine your daily habits. Which ones strengthen your mental resilience? Identify one new habit to incorporate and explain how you will implement it.

Summing Up

Mental strength is a vital attribute that goes far beyond mere toughness or resilience. It's a complex interplay of emotional intelligence, self-control, resilience, and endurance that allows individuals to navigate life's challenges effectively and perform at their best. While genetic factors may influence our baseline capacity for mental strength, it is undoubtedly a skill that can be developed and honed over time. By understanding the components of mental strength and committing to its development, individuals can unlock their full potential and thrive in both their personal and professional lives.

Moving forward, it will be valuable to look at historical lessons and the wisdom passed down through generations. How have boys and men in different cultures and eras built and demonstrated mental strength? What practices and philosophies have stood the test of time in fostering resilience, self-control, and emotional intelligence? Exploring these questions can provide us with timeless strategies for building mental strength.

Chapter 2: The Evolution of Male Mental Toughness

"There is nothing noble in being superior to your fellow man; true nobility is being superior to your former self."
— Ernest Hemingway

Noah and Mike walked out of the gym after basketball practice, the evening air cool against their flushed faces. Noah dribbled the ball absentmindedly, his thoughts clearly elsewhere.

"You know, Mike," Noah began, breaking the silence, "my whole life, people kept telling me to be tough. It's hard to be mentally tough."

Mike nodded, understanding his friend's struggle. "I get it, Noah. It's something that's been expected of men throughout history. We're told to be strong, stoic, and unyielding. But history teaches us that mental strength in boys and men is not solely about toughness or stoicism."

Noah glanced at Mike, curiosity piqued. "What do you mean?"

"It's about embracing authenticity, building connections, and nurturing motivation," Mike explained. "True mental strength involves recognizing and managing your emotions, building strong relationships, and staying motivated even when things get tough."

Noah sighed, "That makes sense, but it still feels so hard. Sometimes I doubt myself, and anxiety takes over. It's like I'm constantly battling my mind."

Mike looked at Noah with empathy. "The truth is, mental strength is a skill that anyone willing to put in the work can learn, hone, and master. Understanding mental strength and supporting those who may be struggling with self-doubt, anxiety, or lack of motivation is crucial in breaking a fixed mindset. These challenges are common and can affect anyone, regardless of age, background, or athletic ability."

Noah nodded slowly. "So, what do we do about it?"

"First, we recognize that willpower and motivation alone are unreliable predictors of success," Mike said. "They can wane over time. What matters more is creating habits and routines that support your goals. It's about consistency, even when you don't feel motivated."

"Yeah, I guess that's true," Noah agreed. "So, it's not just about pushing through with brute force."

"Exactly," Mike confirmed. "It's about being smart with your energy, understanding your limits, and working steadily toward improvement. Mental strength comes from a balance of resilience, emotional intelligence, and the ability to maintain focus over time."

As they walked on, Noah felt a sense of relief. With Mike's support and newfound understanding, he realized that building mental strength was within his reach. It wasn't about being tough all the time but about being consistent, self-aware, and connected with those around him.

...

You might be one of many men like Noah who feel overwhelmed, doubting your ability to handle life's challenges. This chapter will discuss how history teaches us that mental strength in boys and men is not solely about toughness or stoicism. It's about embracing authenticity, building connections, and nurturing motivation.

But the truth is, mental strength is a skill that can be learned and mastered by anyone willing to put in the work. Understanding mental strength and supporting those who may be struggling with self-doubt, anxiety, or lack of motivation is crucial in breaking a fixed mindset. It's important to know that these challenges are common and can affect anyone, regardless of age, background, or athletic ability.

We will explore why willpower and motivation are unreliable predictors of success and how consistent habits and routines play a more significant role in achieving your goals.

Lessons from History

Throughout history, societies have grappled with how best to cultivate mental strength in boys and men. From ancient warrior cultures to modern-day sports psychology, our understanding of mental toughness has evolved significantly. This chapter explores these historical lessons and their relevance to contemporary men seeking to build mental strength.

The Myth of the Stoic Warrior

For centuries, many cultures equated mental strength in men with stoicism and emotional suppression. From Ancient Spartan boys to Roman soldiers all the way into the 20th century... the "strong guy" mentality has been prevalent in many societies.

Imagine being a young Spartan boy in ancient Greece, around the age of seven. You'd be taken from your family and thrown into a harsh training program called the Agoge. This wasn't just a summer camp; it was designed to mold you into a fearless warrior.

One famous story is that of the Spartan soldier Leonidas, who led his men at the Battle of Thermopylae in 480 BCE (Hall, 2023). Despite knowing that they were vastly outnumbered, Leonidas and his warriors stood their ground with bravery and emotional control, embodying the Spartan ideal of mental fortitude

The Spartans believed that to be mentally strong, you had to suppress your emotions and endure physical pain. You'd be taught to bear hunger and cold, and even to sleep on the bare ground. This method wasn't just about becoming strong physically; it was about hardening your mind against weakness. Spartan men were expected to face battle without fear and to remain stoic even in the direst situations

Fast forward a few centuries to ancient Rome, where soldiers were expected to embody the virtues of stoicism and bravery. Roman soldiers like Scipio Africanus were expected to face danger with composure and resilience. Scipio, who led

Roman forces to victory against Hannibal in the Second Punic War, was known for his strategic mind and ability to stay calm under pressure (Scullard, 2024).

The Romans had a concept called virtus, which included bravery and emotional restraint. Soldiers were trained to confront fear without showing it, and to endure the hardships of war with a stiff upper lip. They were taught to be fearless on the battlefield and in all aspects of life.

It does not stop there. In the 19th century, British men were also expected to uphold the "stiff upper lip" mentality. This phrase captured the idea that men should face adversity without showing their emotions.

Winston Churchill became a symbol of this ideal. During World War II, Churchill's leadership embodied the belief that true strength lay in maintaining resolve and not giving in to fear or despair (Meacham, 2018).

The British World War II propaganda phrase "keep calm and carry on" is often associated with Churchill's leadership during the Blitz of 1940. His powerful speeches urged Britain to stand strong and exemplified this era's approach to mental strength. His leadership was about projecting calm and determination to rally the nation through its darkest hours (Irving, 2014).

However, history shows us the limitations of this approach. While the ability to endure hardship is valuable, true mental strength goes far beyond mere stoicism. Many great leaders and athletes throughout history have demonstrated that embracing one's full range of emotions, rather than suppressing them, is key to lasting mental resilience.

Modern Understanding of Mental Strength

The understanding of mental toughness has evolved from the rigid stoicism of the past to a more nuanced view that includes emotional resilience and personal growth. In the 20th century, psychologists such as Abraham Maslow and Carl Jung contributed to this new perspective.

Maslow's Hierarchy of Needs, introduced in 1943, emphasized self-actualization and emotional fulfillment as essential for mental well-being (Mcleod, 2024). Maslow's work introduced the idea that mental strength involves achieving personal growth and fulfilling one's potential rather than just enduring hardship.

Carl Jung's theories in the mid-20th century explored the importance of integrating emotions and personal struggles into one's sense of self (Jung, 1953). Jung's concepts encouraged exploring one's inner life as part of mental resilience.

Today, mental strength is seen as more than just emotional suppression. James Hillman and other modern thinkers have expanded this concept to include emotional intelligence and personal development (D'Heurle, 1975).

James Hillman's book, *The Soul's Code*, argued that mental strength involves understanding and embracing one's emotions and personal challenges (Hillman, 1996). This modern approach encourages seeing mental resilience as a skill that can be developed through introspection and growth. Hillman's work highlights that mental strength involves a dynamic process of personal development rather than a static set of traits.

As you can see, history shows us the limitations of the stoic approach. While the ability to endure hardship is valuable, true mental strength goes far beyond stoicism. Many great leaders and athletes throughout history have demonstrated that embracing one's full range of emotions, rather than suppressing them, is key to lasting mental resilience.

The Power Within

When we think of mental strength, it's easy to picture someone like a stoic warrior or an indomitable athlete. We might believe that mental fortitude is an innate trait reserved for those who seem to have it all together. But here's the truth: mental strength is not a rare gift bestowed upon a few... It's a skill that anyone can learn, practice, and master.

Mental Strength: A Learnable Skill

Imagine mental strength as a muscle. Just as you would train your body to become stronger through exercise, you can train your mind to become more resilient through practice and intentional effort. This idea is crucial to understand because it shifts mental strength from a mysterious, unattainable quality to a series of habits anyone can adopt.

Mental strength is like a set of tools... tools that help you navigate challenges, manage stress, and achieve your goals. If you've ever seen a skilled athlete, a successful businessperson, or a calm parent in a crisis, you've seen someone using these tools effectively. But they didn't start out perfect; they worked on their mental strength just like you can.

Understanding Self-Doubt and Anxiety

Self-doubt and anxiety are universal experiences. They're not signs of weakness but common hurdles that everyone encounters. Understanding this is the first step in breaking free from a fixed mindset that tells you these feelings are insurmountable obstacles.

When it comes to self-doubt, we all have moments when we question our abilities or fear that we're not good enough. This feeling can be paralyzing, but it's important to remember that self-doubt is a normal part of the human experience (Warrell, 2017). Did you know that Tom Brady, now considered one of the greatest quarterbacks, was once drafted in the sixth round and faced doubt from critics? Yet he used this doubt as motivation to prove himself (Cousineau, 2020).

Along with this, anxiety can feel like an overwhelming force, but it's a manageable emotion rather than a permanent state. Strategies like mindfulness and cognitive restructuring can help you address anxiety effectively (Schuman-Olivier, 2020). For example, tennis champion Serena Williams has spoken openly about her struggles with anxiety and how she uses mental techniques to manage her performance on the court (Gallo, 2019).

However, understanding that self-doubt and anxiety are common is just the beginning. You also must see that willpower and motivation alone are unreliable predictors of success. They can get you started, but sustained achievement requires more than just mental toughness.

Why Willpower and Motivation Are Not Enough

We often hear that willpower and motivation are the keys to achieving our goals. While they are important, relying solely on these forces can set us up for disappointment in the long run. Let's explain why willpower and motivation are unreliable predictors of sustained success and what we can do instead.

First off, willpower is not an endless resource. It's like a battery that depletes over time. You can't just power through challenges without giving yourself time to rest, recharge, and practice self-care. Angela Duckworth's *Grit* makes a compelling argument for this point. Duckworth shows that success comes from consistent, long-term effort rather than short bursts of willpower (Duckworth, 2016). If you've ever tried to stick to a diet or a new workout routine just by sheer willpower, you know how quickly that resolve can falter. The trick to lasting success is creating sustainable habits that become part of your routine.

Motivation, on the other hand, is like a fleeting spark. It can ignite your passion for a new project or goal, but it often fades when the initial excitement wears off. James Clear's *Atomic Habits* provides a valuable perspective here, explaining that small, consistent actions lead to real, lasting change, not just temporary bursts of motivation (Clear, 2018). If you've been inspired to start a new habit only to lose interest after a few weeks, you've experienced how unreliable motivation can be.

Building reliable routines and systems, rather than depending on motivation alone, is a more effective approach to achieving long-term success.

Success isn't just about starting strong; it's about persevering through challenges. To achieve your goals, you must develop sustainable habits, build effective routines, and embrace perseverance. Focusing on these strategies will equip you to turn your initial drive into lasting achievement.

Reflection Questions

1. How can the historical examples of mental strength from Spartan warriors or Roman soldiers inform your approach to challenges in your life or sports practice?
2. How can you apply the modern understanding of mental strength, such as emotional intelligence and creating sustainable habits, to improve your performance and well-being in sports or other areas of your life?
3. Reflect on a time when willpower or motivation alone was not enough to reach your goals. What habits or strategies could you have implemented to create a more sustainable path to success?

Summing Up

As Noah and Mike walked away from the gym, the cool evening air brushed against their faces, mirroring the fresh perspective they had just gained. Noah's concerns about mental toughness weren't just his own; they reflected a long history of misconceptions about what it means to be mentally strong. Through their conversation, Mike shed light on a crucial truth: mental strength is about enduring hardship and embracing authenticity, building connections, and nurturing motivation.

As athletes in the modern world, this expanded definition of mental strength is incredibly relevant. It teaches us that mental strength is not about being unbreakable or suppressing feelings. Instead, it's about understanding that self-doubt and anxiety are common experiences, not signs of failure.

For men in sports and beyond, this means embracing a more nuanced view of mental toughness that values emotional intelligence, consistent effort, and personal growth. By moving away from outdated ideals of stoicism and focusing on these modern principles, we can build a more resilient and authentic approach to our challenges. That is why it is so important to develop mental strength. The next chapter will showcase this while teaching us how setbacks fuel improvement.

Chapter 3: Mental Strength as the Answer

"Ultimate vulnerability. That's manly."
– Cameron Conaway, cage fighter

As Mike and Noah walked back to Noah's house, the evening sun dipped below the horizon, casting long shadows across the lawn. Noah tossed the basketball into the garage and grabbed an old baseball and glove from a shelf.

"Hey Mike, you wanna toss the baseball around for a bit?" Noah asked.

"Sure, sounds good," Mike replied, grabbing the glove and stepping into the backyard.

The two friends took their places a good distance apart, Noah winding up for his first throw. As the ball sailed through the air with a satisfying thwack into Mike's glove, Noah's mind wandered back to their conversation from earlier.

"You know, Mike," Noah said as he prepared for another throw, "I've been thinking about our talk on mental strength. Sometimes I wonder if it's really that important. I mean, isn't physical strength and just pushing through challenges enough? I can throw this ball pretty far, but that doesn't feel like it takes much mental strength."

Mike caught the ball and looked at Noah with a knowing smile. "That's an interesting point, Noah. But mental strength is more than just enduring pain or pushing through. It's about how you handle life's ups and downs, both on and off the field."

Noah raised an eyebrow. "Really? I always thought mental strength was just about being tough. I mean, isn't it enough to just be physically strong?"

Mike shook his head, tossing the ball back. "It's true that physical strength is important, but mental strength is crucial for personal growth and long-term success. You see, mental strength isn't just about toughness or ignoring your emotions. It's about understanding your challenges, managing your fears, and using setbacks as opportunities for growth."

Noah caught the ball and threw it back, more thoughtfully this time. "So, you're saying mental strength is more than pushing through hard times?"

Mike nodded, catching the ball with ease. "Exactly. Think about it like this: mental strength helps you respond to challenges effectively, whether you're trying to excel in sports, advance in your career, or navigate personal relationships. It's not just about getting through difficult moments but learning from them and using those lessons to improve."

Noah considered this as he tossed the ball back. "That makes sense. It's not just about being strong; it's about growing from your experiences and staying resilient."

"Right," Mike agreed. "And the prevalent advice often tells us to push through the pain or ignore our emotions. But that doesn't address the root causes of our mental challenges. Instead, developing mental strength means facing your fears, understanding your emotions, and creating habits that support your growth."

Noah nodded, the concept beginning to click. "So, mental strength is more like a set of skills that we can develop rather than just a trait we're born with?"

Mike smiled, tossing the ball back to Noah. "Exactly. It's a skill that anyone can work on. Just like practicing baseball improves your throwing, practicing mental strategies can help you grow stronger mentally. It's about resilience, consistency, and the willingness to work on yourself."

As they continued to toss the baseball, Noah's thoughts turned to the idea that mental strength was not just a fleeting concept but a crucial part of personal development. He realized that building mental strength was essential for achieving his goals and navigating life's challenges beyond physical prowess.

...

Many of us are just like Noah... initially thinking that mental strength isn't all that relevant to sports or that it's simply about physical prowess. It's easy to believe that success in sports comes down to strength, speed, and skill alone, while mental strength seems abstract or secondary. However, this chapter will show that mental strength is relevant and essential for success in sports and beyond.

Mental strength is crucial for athletic achievement and personal growth. Whether you're aiming for success in sports, advancing your career, or simply striving to live a more fulfilling life, the ability to overcome mental obstacles and persist in the face of uncertainty is crucial. This chapter explores why developing mental strength is so important and how setbacks, counterintuitively, can be the very fuel that propels us toward improvement and ultimate success.

The Crucial Role of Mental Strength

Mental strength is the bedrock upon which all other forms of success are built. The inner fortitude helps us rise to challenges and push through obstacles when the going gets tough. Think of mental strength as the invisible force that keeps you moving forward even when you'd rather give up. It allows you to persevere through hardships, maintain your focus and motivation over the long haul, and bounce back from setbacks with renewed determination. It's what allows us to:

1. Persevere when faced with challenges
2. Maintain focus and motivation over long periods
3. Bounce back from failures and setbacks
4. Perform under pressure
5. Adapt to changing circumstances
6. Push beyond our perceived limitations

Imagine you're in the middle of a tough workout. Your muscles are sore, and you're tempted to quit, but your mental strength keeps you going. It's the same in life and sports. When the pressure is on, mental strength helps you perform at your best. It's what lets you stay calm under pressure, adapt to new situations, and push beyond the limits you thought you had

Mental strength is what bridges the gap between

potential and achievement. It's the difference between those who give up when things get tough and those who push through to reach their goals.

Learning from Legends

We already know how Michael Jordan has taught us about mental strength, for example, his incredible ability to perform under pressure and push through personal failures to become a six-time NBA champion. But there are many other sports legends whose stories shine a light on mental strength. Let's look at the lives of a few more remarkable athletes who have shown us what it means to be mentally resilient and how these lessons can inspire us in our own lives.

Serena Williams: Embracing Challenges and Bouncing Back

Serena Williams is a prime example of how mental strength can lead to extraordinary success. Williams has faced numerous challenges throughout her career, including injuries and personal setbacks. Despite these obstacles, she has remained one of the greatest tennis players of all time. Williams has openly discussed her struggles with anxiety and the mental techniques she uses to overcome them. For instance, in the 2018 U.S. Open final, after a series of setbacks and a controversial call from the umpire, Williams rallied to continue competing fiercely, demonstrating resilience and emotional control under immense pressure (Brandman, 2022).

Her ability to confront adversity head-on and her determination to keep improving despite difficulties teach us that mental strength involves bouncing back from failures and continually striving for excellence. Even in recent weeks, Williams continues to inspire us. On X, formerly known as Twitter, Williams posted, "I am not ok today. And that's ok not to be ok. No one is ok every single day. If you are not ok today I'm with you. There's always tomorrow. Love you." (Etienne, 2023).

Muhammad Ali: Courage and Conviction

Muhammad Ali, one of the greatest boxers in history, offers profound lessons on mental strength through his courage and conviction. Ali's career was marked by his physical prowess, mental toughness, and unshakable self-belief. When he was stripped of his titles for refusing to be drafted into the Vietnam War, Ali faced public scorn and legal battles (Brown, 2018). Yet, he maintained his stance with dignity and resilience. Ali famously said, "I hated every minute of training, but I said, 'Don't quit. Suffer now and live the rest of your life as a champion'" (Schlossberg, 2016). His ability to stay true to his principles and his relentless pursuit of his goals despite immense challenges teach us that mental strength involves standing firm in our beliefs and pushing through hardship with resolve.

Tom Brady: The Power of Persistence

Tom Brady's career is a testament to the power of persistence and mental fortitude. Drafted in the sixth round of the 2000 NFL Draft, Brady was not the top prospect. Despite this, he used his perceived failure as motivation to prove himself. Throughout his career, Brady has become one of the most successful quarterbacks in NFL history, with seven Super Bowl victories (DeArdo, 2024). Brady's story teaches us that mental strength is about resilience and the willingness to work harder than anyone else to achieve success. His career reminds us that setbacks are not the end but opportunities to grow stronger and more determined.

David Beckham: Grace Under Pressure

David Beckham's career is a masterclass in handling pressure and bouncing back from setbacks. During the 1998 FIFA World Cup, a controversial red card occurred. Beckham was subjected to intense criticism from fans and the media. But instead of letting this moment of adversity break him, Beckham used it as fuel to push himself harder. Instead, he used it as motivation to improve (Klein, 2018). Beckham's journey teaches us that mental strength is about using challenges as opportunities for growth and staying committed to our goals.

Pelé: Passion and Resilience

Pelé's legendary soccer career shows us the power of passion and resilience. From a young age, Pelé faced obstacles that could have derailed his career. Growing up in poverty, he used soccer as a way to escape his difficult circumstances. Later in life, he encountered challenges like injuries and the pressures of being a global icon (Nelson, 2024). Yet, through it all, Pelé remained focused on his love for the game and his commitment to success. Pelé's story inspires us to embrace our passions and keep pushing forward, no matter our obstacles.

The Problem with "Push Through the Pain"

Despite inspiring stories like these, many men struggle to develop and maintain mental toughness. Part of the problem lies in the advice often given: "Just push through the pain" or "Ignore your emotions and keep going."

While there's value in perseverance, this approach fails to address the root causes of mental challenges. It can lead to suppressing emotions rather than dealing with them constructively. Recent studies have shown that such emotional suppression can actually be counterproductive.

A National Library of Medicine study found that individuals who regularly suppressed their emotions experienced more negative emotions and had lower well-being levels than those who openly expressed their feelings (Srivastava, 2009). This suggests that true mental strength isn't about ignoring our emotions but acknowledging them and learning to manage them effectively.

Shifting Mindsets and Reprogramming Thought Patterns

Developing mental strength isn't about becoming impervious to negative emotions or self-doubt. Instead, it's about shifting our mindset from negativity and self-doubt to positivity and self-belief.

This process involves reprogramming negative thought patterns. For instance, instead of thinking, "I can't do this," a mentally strong person might think, "This is challenging, but I can learn and improve." Instead of "I've failed," they might think, "I haven't succeeded yet."

This shift in thinking isn't about denying reality or ignoring difficulties. It's about framing challenges in a way that empowers us to face them head-on rather than shy away from them.

Embracing Setbacks as Opportunities

The path to developing mental strength isn't always straightforward. It often involves facing our fears, confronting our weaknesses, and pushing beyond our comfort zones. However, as we've seen through examples like Michael Jordan and others, our setbacks and failures often provide the greatest growth opportunities.

By shifting our perspective to view challenges as opportunities rather than obstacles, learning to manage our emotions rather than suppress them, and consistently practicing habits that build mental resilience, we can develop the mental strength needed to overcome any obstacle and achieve our full potential.

Remember, mental strength isn't about never falling down—it's about always getting back up, learning from the experience, and coming back stronger. In the words of Nelson Mandela, "Do not judge me by my successes, judge me by how many times I fell and got back up again."

Reflection Questions

1. Reflect on a personal setback you've experienced. How did you respond, and what did you learn from the experience?
2. Think of a time when you used mental strength to overcome a significant challenge. What strategies did you use to persevere?
3. What are the differences between mental toughness and simply pushing through pain?

Summing Up

As the evening drew to a close, Mike and Noah continued to toss the baseball back and forth, their conversation delving deeper into the essence of mental strength. Noah's initial skepticism about the importance of mental resilience had been met with Mike's thoughtful explanations, revealing that mental strength is much more than enduring pain or ignoring emotions. It is the foundation upon which all other forms of success are built, bridging the gap between our potential and achievements.

Through examples of legendary athletes like Michael Jordan, Serena Williams, Muhammad Ali, and Tom Brady, we've explored how mental strength enables us to persevere through challenges, maintain motivation, and transform setbacks into opportunities for growth. We've seen that true mental resilience involves pushing through tough times, confronting our fears, managing our emotions, and using every experience as a stepping stone toward improvement. In light of this understanding, it's clear that mental strength isn't merely an innate trait but a skill we can develop through practice and dedication.

So, where do we go from here? Having established the significance of mental strength, the next crucial steps are developing self-awareness and adopting a growth mindset. These two concepts are closely linked to the development of mental strength and are essential for turning challenges into growth opportunities.

Chapter 4: Self-Awareness and Growth Mindset

"Failure happens all the time. It happens every day in practice. What makes you better is how you react to it."
– Mia Hamm

    The next day, the sun was high in the sky, casting a warm glow over the tennis courts where Noah and Mike had agreed to meet. The faint sound of tennis balls being struck in the distance, mixed with the chirping of birds, created a pleasant backdrop for their game.

    Noah arrived at the courts first, stretching his arms and glancing around as he waited for Mike. He was feeling a bit nervous, not just because of the game but also because he wasn't very confident in his tennis skills. Mike's presence was reassuring, though, and he looked forward to spending time with his friend.

    A few minutes later, Mike pulled up, his tennis gear in tow. After a quick greeting and a brief catch-up on their day, the two friends headed to the nearest court. Mike set up the tennis balls and rackets, and they began to warm up.

    "Alright, let's start with some light rallies," Mike said, tossing a ball to Noah.

Noah took the ball and tossed it back, but his shots were a bit off. He missed a few, and his movements felt awkward. After a few minutes, Noah sighed and said, "You know, Mike, I'm not sure why I agreed to this. I've always been terrible at tennis. I think I'm just not cut out for it."

Mike paused and looked at Noah thoughtfully. "Really? What makes you say that?"

Noah shrugged. "I've tried playing before, and it never goes well. I think I'm just bad at it, and that's just how it is."

Mike nodded, but a small smile played on his lips. "You know, Noah, that's actually a common way of thinking. It's called a fixed mindset, where you believe your abilities are set in stone and can't change them."

Noah looked puzzled. "A fixed mindset?"

"Yeah," Mike explained. "A fixed mindset is when you see your talents and intelligence as static. You think you're either good at something or not, and failures are seen as proof that you're just not cut out for it."

Noah frowned as he hit another errant shot. "So, what's the alternative?"

Mike tossed the ball back to him. "The alternative is a growth mindset. With a growth mindset, you see challenges as opportunities to learn and improve. Instead of thinking you're bad at something and that's the end, you believe you can get better with effort and practice."

Noah raised an eyebrow. "So, you're saying that just because I'm not good at tennis now doesn't mean I can't get better?"

"Exactly!" Mike said enthusiastically. "A growth mindset means you embrace challenges and view setbacks as chances to learn. Instead of saying, 'I'm bad at tennis,' you can say, 'I'm not very good at tennis yet, but I can improve with practice.' It's all about seeing failure as a stepping stone rather than a permanent state."

Noah thought about this briefly, taking a deep breath before hitting the ball back to Mike with more intent. "Okay, so how do I start developing a growth mindset?"

Mike took a moment to demonstrate a proper tennis swing, explaining as he went: "It starts with self-awareness. Recognize where you're struggling and acknowledge that it's okay not to be perfect at everything immediately. From there, you focus on learning and practicing rather than just judging yourself."

Noah nodded, beginning to see the value in this new perspective. "So, I should focus on improving rather than just being frustrated with how bad I am?"

"Exactly," Mike confirmed. "For example, if you miss a shot, instead of thinking, 'I'm terrible at this,' think about what you can learn from that mistake. Maybe your form was off, or you need to practice your aim. Use it as a chance to grow."

Noah smiled as he began hitting the ball more consistently. "That makes a lot of sense. I guess I was just so focused on being perfect that I forgot to enjoy the process of getting better."

"That's a great attitude," Mike said, grinning. "It's all about embracing the challenges and seeing them as opportunities to grow."

Noah's shots became steadier as they continued to play, and he enjoyed the game more. The conversation with Mike had shifted his perspective on tennis and challenges in general.

By the time they finished their match, Noah felt a renewed sense of enthusiasm for tennis and for tackling other areas of his life where he had previously been stuck. "Thanks for the lesson, Mike. I feel like I better understand how to approach things now."

Mike clapped him on the back. "Anytime, Noah. Remember, a growth mindset can change how you handle challenges on the court and in life."

As they walked off the court, the sun began to set, casting a golden light over their conversation. Noah was excited to apply what he had learned to other areas of his life, knowing that with a growth mindset, every setback could become a chance for improvement.

...

Like Noah, many of us deal with fixed mindsets without realizing it. Have you ever avoided trying something new because you didn't think you'd be good at it? Or have you found yourself feeling discouraged when you face a challenge? These common experiences reflect a fixed mindset, where we believe our abilities are unchangeable.

In this chapter, we will go over how to break free from this mindset and develop a growth mindset instead. We'll glance at the power of self-awareness, which is the first step in managing your emotions effectively and understanding how your thoughts shape your actions. You'll learn how a growth mindset—believing your abilities can be developed through dedication and hard work—can transform your approach to challenges. We will also discuss practical strategies for cultivating this mindset, the role of self-compassion in maintaining it, and how to turn these insights into actionable steps for success in your personal and professional life.

The Power of Self-Awareness

Self-awareness is recognising and understanding one's thoughts, feelings, and motivations (Cherry 2024). It is like having an internal mirror that allows you to see yourself clearly, including your strengths, weaknesses, beliefs, and values. Self-awareness is the first step in managing one's emotions effectively and making conscious choices about one's behavior.

To develop self-awareness, you need to practice a few key habits. Start by paying attention to your thoughts and emotions throughout the day. Reflect on your experiences to understand how you react to different situations. Don't hesitate to seek feedback from those around you—they might offer insights you hadn't considered. Mindfulness practices, like meditation, can also help you stay present and aware. Keeping a journal or engaging in regular self-reflection exercises allows you to explore your inner world more deeply (Cherry 2024).

Cultivating self-awareness is the first step in breaking free from limiting beliefs and negative self-talk that might hold you back. For instance, if you find yourself constantly thinking, "I'm not good enough" or "I can't do this," these negative patterns can seriously affect your performance and overall well-being. By developing a deeper understanding of yourself, you can challenge these thoughts and shift your mindset toward growth and improvement.

The Growth Mindset: A Game-Changer

Once you've developed self-awareness, the next step is to cultivate a growth mindset. This concept, pioneered by psychologist Carol Dweck, is based on the belief that your abilities and intelligence can be developed through dedication and hard work (Dweck, 2016).

The power of a growth mindset was further underscored by Dr. Angela Duckworth's pioneering research on "grit." In her study at the University of Pennsylvania, Duckworth found that mental toughness, or "grit" as she calls it, is a better predictor of success than IQ, talent, or any other factor (Duckworth, 2016).

Duckworth's research showed that people with high levels of grit were more likely to persevere in the face of adversity, bounce back from setbacks, and achieve their long-term goals. This highlights the crucial role that mindset plays in achieving success and developing mental strength.

Fixed vs. Growth Mindsets

A growth mindset contrasts sharply with a fixed mindset, which assumes that your talents and intelligence are static and cannot be changed. People with a fixed mindset often avoid challenges, give up easily, and feel threatened by the success of others (Cote, 2022).

Those with a fixed mindset often see their abilities as predetermined and rigid, leading them to avoid challenges for fear of failure, give up more easily when faced with obstacles, and feel threatened or envious of others' achievements. They might think, "I'm just not good at this," or "I'll never be as talented as they are," which can prevent them from taking risks or pushing their limits.

People with a fixed mindset may also be more likely to react defensively to criticism, seeing it as a personal attack rather than a chance for growth. This mindset can lead to a fear of failure that stifles their potential and keeps them from reaching their goals (Cote, 2022). For example, a young athlete with a fixed mindset might avoid practicing a difficult skill because they believe they lack the innate talent to master it. In contrast, an athlete with a growth mindset would embrace the challenge, understanding that practice and perseverance can lead to improvement.

Moreover, a fixed mindset often causes individuals to view their failures as reflections of their inadequacies rather than learning experiences. For instance, if a tennis player loses a match, a fixed mindset might lead them to think, "I'm just not cut out for this," whereas a growth mindset would encourage them to analyze what went wrong, learn from the experience, and try again with renewed strategies.

Here's a detailed list of fixed vs. growth mindset examples in sports, showing how different attitudes can affect performance and development. Please be mindful that these examples are closely related to affirmations, which we will discuss in further detail in the next chapter. Our internal dialogue has a huge impact on our actions and beliefs, which in turn fuels our mindsets.

Fixed Mindset	Growth Mindset
"I'm just not good at this sport."	"I'm not great at this yet, but I can improve with practice."
"I lost the game because I'm not talented enough."	"I lost the game, but I can learn from my mistakes and get better."
"I can't improve my skills; I'm too old for this."	"Age doesn't limit my ability to improve. I can always develop new skills."
"If I have to work hard, I must not be good enough."	"Hard work is part of the process to get better. I'm willing to put in the effort."
"I'm only as good as my last performance."	"Every performance is a learning opportunity, regardless of the outcome."
"I'm afraid to try new techniques because I might fail."	"Trying new techniques is a chance to learn and grow, even if I fail at first."
"If I'm not the best, there's no point in trying."	"Being the best isn't the goal. Improvement and effort are what matter."
"I don't want to play against better players; I might embarrass myself."	"Playing against better players is a chance to learn and improve my own skills."
"I'm just not a natural athlete."	"Athletic ability can be developed through practice and perseverance."
"I can't change how I play; this is just who I am."	"I can always refine and adjust my game to become a better player."
"I avoid challenges to avoid failure."	"Challenges help me grow and become a stronger athlete."
"I only practice when I feel motivated."	"I practice regularly to build discipline and improve, regardless of how motivated I feel."
"I don't like to practice skills that I'm not immediately good at."	"I see practicing challenging skills as an opportunity to grow and improve."
"I get discouraged when I see others succeed."	"I use others' successes as inspiration and motivation for my own goals."

Now that we've explored the differences between a fixed mindset and a growth mindset, you might be wondering, "How do I develop a growth mindset?" The answer lies in actively practicing self-awareness, embracing challenges, and reprogramming your thought patterns.

Cultivating a Growth Mindset

Thankfully, cultivating a growth mindset is not as hard as it might seem.
The first step is to embrace challenges instead of shying away from them (Gupta, 2024). Each obstacle is an opportunity to learn and grow. For example, don't avoid hilly courses if you're a runner. Instead, you can see them as a chance to enhance your endurance and technique.

Next, it's important to reframe failure. Instead of viewing it as a reflection of your abilities, see it as a learning experience. Ask yourself, "What can I learn from this?" After a setback, spend time analyzing what went wrong and how you can do better next time.

Additionally, focus on the process rather than just the outcome. While goals are important, fixating on results can be counterproductive. Shift your attention to the journey of improvement. Celebrate the effort you put in, the strategies you're learning, and the progress you're making, no matter how small it may seem (Davis, 2024).

Another effective strategy is to harness the power of the word "yet." When you catch yourself thinking, "I can't do this," add "yet" to the end of the sentence. This simple adjustment transforms a statement of defeat into a declaration of potential. For example, "I can't master this technique... yet" acknowledges your current limitations while keeping the door open for growth.

Cultivating a love for learning is also essential. Approach each practice session, game, or competition as an opportunity to discover something new. Maintain curiosity about your sport or field, and always look for ways to deepen your understanding and refine your skills (Davis, 2024).

Embracing criticism is another crucial aspect of a growth mindset. Instead of becoming defensive when receiving feedback, view it as valuable information for improvement. Thank others for their input and reflect on how to use it to boost your performance.

Finally, find inspiration in others' success. Instead of feeling threatened by others' achievements, let their stories motivate you. Study successful individuals in your field and learn from their experiences to inspire your growth (Gupta, 2024).

If you throw these strategies into your mindset, you'll be well on your way to developing a growth mindset that drives you toward success and personal development.

The Role of Self-Compassion

While pushing yourself to improve is key, don't forget to cut yourself some slack! Being kind to yourself can make a big difference, especially when things go awry. Research shows that self-compassion can ignite motivation, build emotional resilience, and fuel personal growth (Chen, 2018). So, the next time you're feeling down, give yourself a mental high-five and remember: it's okay to be a work in progress! Here are some ways to practice self-compassion…

1. Remember that making mistakes and facing setbacks is a universal human experience. You're not alone in your struggles (Lieberman, 2018).
2. Pay attention to your inner dialogue. Would you speak to a friend the way you speak to yourself? If not, try to adopt a more supportive and encouraging tone.
3. Practice being present and aware of your thoughts and feelings without judgment. This can help you respond to difficulties with greater clarity and compassion.

While striving for growth is important, you should also learn to accept yourself as you are in the present moment. Remember, you are worthy of respect and kindness regardless of your achievements or failures.

Turning Insights into Action

Understanding these concepts is just the first step. The real power comes from putting them into practice.

Here are some actionable steps you can take to apply these insights in your life and sport:

Strategy	Details
Daily Reflection	Set aside time daily to reflect on your thoughts, actions, and experiences. What challenges did you face? How did you respond? What can you learn from these experiences?
Set Process Goals	Alongside your outcome goals, set process goals focusing on the actions and habits that will lead to improvement. For example, if your outcome goal is to run a marathon, a process goal might be to follow your training plan consistently.
Celebrate Effort and Progress	Make a habit of acknowledging your efforts and the progress you've made, no matter how small. This reinforces the value of hard work and perseverance.
Seek Out Challenges	Regularly step out of your comfort zone. This could mean trying a new training technique, competing at a higher level, or taking on a leadership role in your team.
Practice Positive Self-Talk	Pay attention to your inner dialogue and consciously replace negative self-talk with more supportive and growth-oriented language. In the next chapter, we will explore this concept further.
Learn from Role Models	Identify individuals in your sport or field who embody a growth mindset. Study their approaches to challenges and setbacks and try to emulate their mindset.

When you constantly work on your mindset, you can develop the mental strength to overcome obstacles and reach your full potential in sports and life. Remember, developing a growth mindset is a journey, not a destination. Be patient with yourself and enjoy the process of continuous growth and improvement.

Reflection Questions

1. How can developing a growth mindset change your approach to challenges in your own life?
2. Reflect on a time when you had a fixed mindset about a skill or ability. How did this mindset affect your efforts and outcomes?
3. What are some ways you can practice self-awareness when facing setbacks or failures?

Summing Up

Developing self-awareness, cultivating a growth mindset, and practicing self-compassion lay the foundation for unshakeable mental strength. These tools allow you to identify and challenge limiting beliefs, embrace challenges as opportunities for growth, and treat yourself with kindness as you navigate the ups and downs of your journey.

Remember, developing mental strength requires consistent effort and practice. But with each step you take, each challenge you face, and each setback you overcome, you're building the mental resilience needed to achieve your full potential.

In the following chapters, we'll explore strategies and techniques that top athletes and high-performers use to master their mental game. But it all starts here, with understanding yourself and embracing a mindset of growth and possibilities. Are you ready to unleash your inner warrior?

Chapter 5: What's Really Holding You Back?

"Somebody gives you an opportunity, say yes to it. So what if you fail? you won't know if you fail or succeed unless you try."
– Ann Meyers

So, Noah and Mike rode their bikes along a well-worn trail on the next crisp Saturday morning. The sun was shining, and the sounds of nature and the occasional clink of their bike gears filled the air. As they approached a fast-flowing stream of water covering their path, Noah slowed down and stopped. He looked at the water and then at Mike, who had also stopped beside him.

"Shoot. Let's turn around," Noah said.

"Really? Why don't we jump the bikes over it? It's not that big."

Noah felt a pang of fear and self-doubt, unsure if he had the skills or confidence to make the jump. The stream was wider than he had ever biked over before, and if he were to misjudge his landing, he could get seriously hurt. He nervously shifted his weight from one foot to the other. "I don't know, man," he said.

Mike gave him a reassuring smile. "What's holding you back from reaching your full potential?" he asked, his tone gentle yet probing. "Is it fear of failure, self-doubt, or just a lack of confidence?"

Noah looked at the fast-running water and then at Mike, unsure what to say. "I guess I'm afraid I might mess up," he admitted, feeling vulnerable. "I'm not sure if I can actually make it."

Mike nodded, understanding the struggle. "We all have fears and doubts," he said. "But that's the first step toward overcoming them. Positive self-talk and mindfulness can help you break through those barriers. Just like you train your body to get stronger, you can train your mind to build resilience and confidence."

Noah listened intently as Mike continued. "You have the power to face your fears, and you can find the courage to jump over that river. It's about taking small steps, believing in yourself, and knowing that you can grow and improve."

Mike's words resonated with Noah as he considered what was possible. "Think of this river as a metaphor for the challenges you face in life," Mike said. "Whether you aim to improve in a sport or simply look to live a more fulfilling life, the path to success begins with a commitment to yourself and a willingness to work through your fears."

Noah took a deep breath and nodded slowly. He realized that overcoming his fear of moving water blocking his path was more than just about making the jump; it was about confronting his self-doubt and building mental strength. With newfound determination, he prepared himself for the jump, ready to embrace the challenge as a step toward his personal growth.

...

We all have moments like Noah. We feel scared and uncertain, not knowing what to do. Luckily, Noah eventually understood that developing mental strength was a journey that began with small, brave steps. This story can serve as an example of how we should commit to facing fears, practicing resilience, and believing in our potential. The path to achieving our goals, whether in sports or life, starts with a single leap of faith.

In this chapter, we'll explore the common obstacles to reaching our full potential and discuss strategies for overcoming them. Remember, identifying these barriers is the first step toward conquering them.

The Fear Factor

Fear of failure, self-doubt, and lack of confidence are some of the biggest obstacles we face on the road to success. These fears can keep us stuck in our comfort zones and stop us from taking risks that could lead to growth.

But here's the truth: everyone feels fear. It's not something to be ashamed of. What matters is how we handle it. Instead of letting fear hold you back, try to see it as a sign that you're stepping out of your comfort zone and making progress (Wilson, 2020).

Here's a practical tip: the next time fear starts to creep in, take a moment to notice it. Don't let it control you... acknowledge that it's there, and then ask yourself, "What's the worst that could happen?" Often, you'll realize that the risks are smaller than you imagined and that the potential rewards are worth taking the chance (Perry, 2022).

So next time fear tries to hold you back, flip the script. See it as a sign you're about to stretch your limits, and remember that the best growth happens outside of your comfort zone. Embrace the challenge and move forward with courage!

A Comparison Trap

In today's hyper-connected world, it's easy to fall into the comparison trap. You know what I mean: when you're scrolling through the rabbit-hole of social media, you will most likely think more than just "liking" your friends' posts. The truth is that many of us compare ourselves to them, which can make us feel like we're not measuring up.

Here's a fact: constant comparison can make us unhappy. Research shows that comparing ourselves to others can lead to feelings of inadequacy and decreased life satisfaction (Lee, 2020). Everyone's journey is different, and success looks different for each person. What might seem like a perfect life on Instagram is often just one small part of the bigger picture.

Instead of comparing yourself to others, try focusing on your own progress and growth. Everyone has their own path, and it's important to measure your success by your own standards.

One way to avoid this is to set personal benchmarks based on your past achievements rather than comparing yourself to others. Track your improvements and celebrate your successes, no matter how small they might seem. For example, if you ran a mile in 10 minutes last year and now can do it in 9 minutes, that's progress! Acknowledge these achievements and use them as motivation for future goals.

The Comfort Zone Conundrum

Growth happens outside our comfort zones, but it's natural to want to stay in our safe and familiar spaces. Believe it or not, staying in our comfort zones can lead to stagnation and missed growth opportunities. While stepping out of these safe spaces might feel uncomfortable, it's where real growth happens.

You don't have to make big changes all at once. In fact, gradual steps are often more effective. You don't need to make drastic changes overnight to see results. Rather, you can challenge yourself to do one thing each day that pushes you slightly out of your comfort zone. It could be something as simple as trying a new workout routine or starting a conversation with a stranger at the gym. These small actions can help you grow and become more comfortable with change. By making a habit of stepping outside your comfort zone, you open yourself up to new opportunities and experiences that can lead to personal and professional growth.

Becoming Your Own Cheerleader

Our internal dialogue has a huge impact on our actions

and beliefs. The way we talk to ourselves can either lift us up or hold us back. Studies show that negative self-talk can reinforce limiting beliefs, increase stress, and decrease motivation, all of which make it harder to achieve our goals (Kim et al. 2021). In this way, developing positive self-talk is a bit like building muscle. It takes regular practice. Just as you would work out to build physical strength, you need to work on your inner dialogue to strengthen your mindset (Scott, 2023).

What Are Positive and Negative Affirmations?

Positive Affirmations are statements that support your goals and reinforce a healthy mindset (Uhrig, 2020). They are uplifting and encourage you to focus on your strengths and potential. For instance, saying, "I am improving every day" helps you acknowledge your progress and stay motivated.

Negative Affirmations are self-critical statements that can undermine your confidence and reinforce limiting beliefs (Davis, 2023). These thoughts often start with "I can't" or "I'm not good enough," and they can lead to increased anxiety and decreased motivation. For example, saying, "I always mess up under pressure" can create a self-fulfilling prophecy.

If you look back to our discussion about fixed and growth mindsets, you will learn more about why it is so important to reframe the way you think about yourself. We have already explored some great examples of positive and negative self-talk in relation to growth and fixed mindsets because these two concepts are closely connected. Self-talk plays a crucial role in reinforcing either a growth or fixed mindset. The examples of positive and negative mindset strategies you've seen are more than just words, they reflect these overarching affirmations.

Ultimately, by focusing on positive self-talk, you can gradually change your beliefs and actions to better align with your potential and aspirations.

Staying Present and Focused With Mindfulness

Mindfulness is the practice of being fully present and engaged in the moment, without judgment or distraction (Lynch, 2012). It involves paying attention to your thoughts, feelings, and surroundings with a sense of curiosity and acceptance. While it sounds simple, mindfulness can be a powerful tool for reducing stress, improving focus, and enhancing overall well-being.

At its core, mindfulness encourages you to observe your experiences without letting them overwhelm or define you. In sports, mindfulness can help you stay calm under pressure, stay focused on your training goals, and bounce back from setbacks. It's about acknowledging your thoughts and emotions without getting caught up in them. This approach helps you to respond to situations more thoughtfully rather than reacting impulsively. Research shows that mindfulness can improve mental health by reducing symptoms of anxiety and depression and increasing emotional resilience (Keng, Smoski, & Robbins, 2013). Here are some effective strategies to help you incorporate mindfulness into your daily life and in sports.

Strategy	Description	Tips
Mindful Breathing	Focusing on your breath to center your mind (Greater Good Science Center, 2023).	Start with a few minutes a day and gradually increase the time. Use it before games or practice to calm your nerves.
Body Scan Meditation	Paying attention to physical sensations in different parts of your body (Smookler, 2023).	Aim for a 10-15-minute session, lying down or sitting. Perform this exercise after intense sessions to check for muscle tension.
Mindful Eating	Being present and attentive during meals (Mayo Clinic Staff, 2023).	Avoid distractions like TV; savor each bite. Practice to ensure proper nutrition and fuel for training.
Mindful Walking	Paying attention to the sensations and surroundings during a walk.	Practice during your daily walks or as a mindful break.
Mindful Observation	Observing details of an object or scene without judgment.	Focus on details; appreciate the present moment. Use it to reflect on training sessions and boost motivation.
Gratitude Journaling	Writing down things you're grateful for.	Write down three things daily; focus on genuine appreciation.
Mindful Listening	Giving full attention to the person you're communicating with (Lunch, 2012).	Listen without interrupting; notice non-verbal cues.

By integrating these mindfulness techniques into your sports routine, you can build mental resilience, stay focused, and enhance your performance both on and off the field.

Reflection Questions

1. What's one fear that's been holding you back? How can you reframe it as an opportunity for growth?
2. What's one small step you can take today to push beyond your comfort zone?
3. How can you incorporate a brief mindfulness practice into your daily routine?

Summing Up

Remember, you have the power to develop the mental strength and resilience needed to achieve your goals. It all starts with a few key practices. Begin by facing your fears and seeing them as chances for growth rather than obstacles. Focus on your own progress instead of comparing yourself to others, and make a habit of stepping out of your comfort zone with small, consistent challenges. Develop positive self-talk to boost your confidence and replace negative thoughts. Finally, practice mindfulness to stay present and focused. The journey to mental strength starts with a commitment to yourself, a willingness to work, and a belief in your potential. In the next chapter, we will talk about techniques to harness inner strength and achieve peak performance.

Chapter 6: Unlocking Peak Performance

"Many times, I had to dig deep and perform. All of that adversity helped me and drove me to want to be the best."
—Hayley Wickenheiser

Noah walked through the front door of his apartment, his shoulders sagging under the weight of another long day at work. His mind was already drifting to the comfort of the couch, where he planned to unwind with a bag of chips and a cold soda. He had been looking forward to this moment all day, imagining how good it would feel to sink into the cushions and let the stresses of work fade away.

He was just about to head to the kitchen when his phone buzzed. Glancing at the screen, he saw Mike's name flashing. With a sigh, he answered the call.

"Hey, Mike. What's up?"

"Hey, Noah! I was just about to head out for a run. Want to join me?" Mike's voice was upbeat and full of energy.

"A run? You must be feeling super motivated. How do you always manage to stay so driven?"

"It's not just about motivation, dude. It's about adopting the right mindset and habits. I've been working hard on developing what they call the 'seven traits of mentally strong people.'"

Noah raised an eyebrow, now staring at the bag of chips on the kitchen counter. "Seven traits? What are those?"

"Well, the first trait is facing reality and challenges directly. It means not avoiding problems but confronting them head-on. For instance, I used to skip workouts when I was tired, but now I face the challenge and stick to my routine."

This made Noah shift his gaze away from the tempting chips. He began to pace the room as he listened. "Okay, what's the next one?"

"The second trait is accepting responsibility for choices," Mike continued. "It's about owning up to your decisions and their outcomes. I used to blame my schedule for not exercising, but I realized it was up to me to make time."

"That makes sense," Noah said. "What about the third one?"

"The third trait is self-monitoring and self-correcting," Mike said. "It's being aware of your actions and adjusting when necessary. For example, if I'm not making progress, I review my training and tweak it for better results."

"I see. And the fourth?"

"Finding meaning in past experiences," Mike said. "I look at my past failures as learning opportunities. For instance, when I miss a goal, I analyze what went wrong and use that knowledge to improve. The next one? It's balancing emotions and facts. It means not letting emotions cloud your judgment.

For instance, if I'm frustrated with my progress, I focus on the facts and my long-term goals rather than just my current feelings."

"No wonder you're so driven," Noah said. "What's the sixth trait?"

"Addressing past traumas," Mike said. "I work through my past issues rather than letting them hold me back. It's about acknowledging past setbacks and using them as a source of strength. After that, it's all about demonstrating emotional intelligence," Mike said. "It's about understanding and managing your emotions and others'. I use this trait to keep a positive mindset and communicate effectively with my training partners."

Noah was impressed. "It sounds like you've put in a lot of work. How did you get started with all of this?"

Mike chuckled. "I started by learning about these traits and then incorporating them into my routine. For instance, I use visualization exercises to see myself achieving my goals. I also practice positive self-talk to stay motivated."

"It's pretty inspiring, Mike. I guess I've been letting my self-doubt hold me back. Maybe I should try some of these techniques."

"Absolutely! You can start by visualizing your goals, setting small, achievable targets, and being patient with yourself. It's all about creating lasting change and consistently working toward improvement."

Noah looked at the couch, then at. "You know what? I think I'll take you up on that run. Let's do this."

Mike grinned. "Awesome! I'll meet you outside in ten minutes!"

...

Just like Mike and Noah discovered, reaching peak performance requires more than just motivation; it demands a deliberate journey of practice and dedication. This chapter will explore how developing mental strength involves consistently applying the top seven traits of mentally strong people... such as facing reality, accepting responsibility, and balancing emotions. These traits are essential for overcoming obstacles and achieving your highest potential. In your mental gymnasium, you have many "tools" at your disposal for growth and improvement, including visualization techniques, positive self-talk, and strategies to build focus.

The Top Seven Traits of Mentally Strong People

Developing mental strength is a journey that requires consistent practice and dedication. Mentally strong people demonstrate seven key traits: they face reality and challenges directly, accept responsibility for their choices, self-monitor and self-correct their behavior, find meaning in past experiences, balance emotions with facts, and address past traumas instead of burying them (Sangerma, 2023). These traits are closely linked to emotional intelligence and resilience, which are essential for overcoming obstacles and achieving peak performance. Believe it or not, many athletes possess these traits. Let's talk a little bit about each and consider what sports stars can teach us about them.

1. Facing Reality and Challenges Directly

Mentally strong athletes confront problems rather than avoid or deny them. They assess situations based on facts and seek solutions. Serena Williams, as we know, confronted her injuries and setbacks directly by seeking medical advice, adjusting her training, and focusing on rehabilitation to return to peak form (Brandman, 2022).

2. Accepting Responsibility for Choices

Mentally resilient athletes take ownership of their decisions and their outcomes, rather than blaming external factors for their failures. Michael Jordan, who we have mentioned before in this book, took responsibility for his early career setbacks. He worked on his skills and leadership to overcome challenges and achieve greatness (Piccotti, 2023).

3. Self-Monitoring and Self-Correcting

This trait involves being aware of one's own thoughts, behaviors, and feelings, and making adjustments to improve performance. Tom Brady, renowned for his NFL success, consistently monitors his performance through video analysis and adjusts his techniques to maintain high standards (DeArdo, 2024).

4. Finding Meaning in Past Experiences

Mentally strong athletes use their past experiences, including failures, as learning opportunities and sources of inspiration. Simone Biles, one of the most decorated gymnasts, viewed her past competitive struggles as valuable lessons that contributed to her growth and eventual success.

5. Balancing Emotions and Facts

This trait involves separating emotions from objective reality to maintain focus and make rational decisions. Rafael Nadal, a top tennis player, demonstrates this trait by focusing on his game strategy rather than letting frustration from mistakes affect his performance (Nicola, 2022).

6. Addressing Past Traumas

Mentally strong athletes confront and work through past traumas instead of letting them hinder their current performance. Andre Agassi, a former tennis champion, dealt with personal traumas by seeking therapy and addressing these issues, which helped him overcome obstacles and achieve success (Santa Florentina, 2016).

7. Demonstrating Emotional Intelligence

This trait involves understanding and managing one's own emotions and recognizing others' emotions to build positive relationships and effective teams. Coach Phil Jackson, known for his success with the Chicago Bulls and LA Lakers, used emotional intelligence to manage team dynamics and foster a strong, cohesive group (Dalaney, 2023).

Now that you understand these seven traits... How on Earth do you get there? Well, there are a bunch of exercises you can use to build mental strength. Think of it like your mind's gymnasium, where you have your pick of tools that can help you meet your goals.

The Mind's Gymnasium

Mental strength, like physical strength, can be developed through consistent practice and targeted exercises. Individuals can use techniques like visualization to enhance performance, positive self-talk to boost confidence, and a "funnel" to stay focused. Embracing these practices helps train the mind, much like physical exercise trains the body. By implementing these strategies, you'll be able to push your boundaries, overcome obstacles, and reach new heights in your personal and professional pursuits.

Sculpting Mental Muscles with Visualization

Visualization, also known as mental rehearsal or imagery, is a powerful technique used by elite athletes to enhance performance. Research has shown that mental practice can be almost as effective as physical practice in improving skills and performance. A groundbreaking study by Dr. Biasiotto at the University of Chicago found that basketball players who visualized free throws for 20 minutes a day improved their accuracy by 23% after just 20 days, without any physical practice (Cicio, 2024). This demonstrates the profound impact that mental training can have on physical performance.

The power of visualization lies in its ability to activate the same neural pathways in the brain that are used during actual physical performance. When you vividly imagine yourself executing a skill or achieving a goal, your brain forms and strengthens the neural connections associated with that action, making it easier to perform in reality.

So... how do you do this?

Start with 10-15 minutes daily to visualization practice. Find a quiet, comfortable space where you won't be disturbed. Close your eyes and begin by taking a few deep breaths to relax your body and mind. Then, start to visualize yourself successfully performing your sport or task. Engage all your senses:

1. See yourself in vivid detail, from your surroundings to your movements.
2. Hear the sounds associated with your performance - the crowd, the impact of a ball, your own breathing.
3. Feel the sensations in your body as you move and execute your skills.
4. Smell and taste the environment if relevant (e.g., the scent of grass on a soccer field).

The more vivid and detailed your visualization, the more effective it will be. Practice visualizing both perfect performances and successfully overcoming challenges. This will prepare you mentally for various scenarios you might encounter.

The Self-Talk Symphony

While our previous discussions on the inner voice, affirmations, and growth mindset touch on similar concepts, self-talk deserves its own focus because it directly impacts our day-to-day reactions and decisions.

Unlike affirmations, which are positive statements like "I am strong," self-talk is the broader practice of our internal dialogue, including both negative and positive thoughts (Wong, 2023). While a growth mindset is about believing in our ability to improve through effort, self-talk is the active process of applying that mindset in real-time situations. Inner voice refers to the general self-narrative, whereas self-talk is about how we consciously manage our thoughts in the moment.

For example, if an athlete thinks, "I can't win," their self-talk can shift to, "I've prepared for this, and I'm ready." This shift from negative to positive self-talk boosts confidence and performance. There are several types of effective self-talk (Singh, 2020):

1. Instructional self-talk: Giving yourself specific directions or cues (e.g., "Keep your eye on the ball")
2. Motivational self-talk: Encouraging yourself (e.g., "You've got this!")
3. Mood-related self-talk: Managing your emotional state (e.g., "Stay calm and focused")

So, do your best to develop a set of positive, present-tense affirmations related to your goals. For example, "I am strong and capable" or "I perform well under pressure." Repeat these affirmations daily, especially before challenging tasks or competitions. Remember, changing your self-talk patterns takes time and consistent effort. Be patient with yourself and celebrate small improvements along the way.

The Focus Funnel

Concentration and focus are crucial for peak performance. The ability to maintain attention to relevant cues while ignoring distractions can make the difference between success and failure in high-pressure situations.

A study on Olympic athletes found that the ability to focus attention was one of the key mental skills that distinguished medalists from non-medalists (Gould, 1988). This highlights the critical role that attention control plays in achieving elite performance. Focus is not just about concentrating harder; it's about directing your attention efficiently and effectively (Skidmore, 2023). This involves:

1. Selective attention: Focusing on relevant cues and ignoring distractions
2. Sustained attention: Maintaining focus over time
3. Divided attention: Managing multiple tasks or stimuli when necessary
4. Shifting attention: Flexibly moving your focus as needed

You can improve your focus in many ways. You can start by minimizing distractions in your environment during practice and performance. Try using cue words or phrases to quickly bring your attention back when it wanders. Also, try task-specific concentration exercises (e.g., juggling for hand-eye coordination) to gradually increase the duration and complexity of your focus over time.

Reflection Questions

1. Which of the seven traits of mentally strong people resonates most with you?
2. Which of these techniques can you apply to your daily routine today?
3. What are three positive self-talk statements you can use to boost your confidence?

Summing Up

Developing mental strength is a journey that requires consistent practice and dedication. The top seven traits of mentally strong people—such as facing reality, accepting responsibility, and balancing emotions—are crucial for overcoming challenges and achieving peak performance. To develop these strengths, there are many "tools" in your "mental gymnasium" that you can use to practice and reach that goal. Visualization, positive self-talk, and building focus are all techniques and are just a few of the many ways to do this. Next, we will learn about another tool, the Mental Rehearsal Method.

Chapter 7: The Mental Rehearsal Method

"I never hit a shot, not even in practice, without having a very sharp in-focus picture of it in my head."
-Jack Nicklaus

A few weeks later, a group of friends invited Mike and Noah out to the beach. As fate would have it, everyone decided to play a round of beach volleyball. Noah found himself standing on the volleyball court, staring at the net with excitement and dread.

"Yo man," Mike said as he began to warm up. "What's on your mind?"

"Well, I guess I'm just nervous. I've been practicing a lot, but I'm worried I might choke during the matches. I just don't know how to get past this fear."

Mike responded quickly, "I get that. I used to have the same issue before games, whether it was a competition or just playing with friends. But I found something that really helped me—have you heard of the Mental Rehearsal Method?"

"No, I haven't. What's that?"

Mike served the volleyball to another player waiting nearby and continued, "It's a technique where you mentally rehearse your performance. You picture yourself in the game, seeing yourself succeed and handling challenges. It's all about visualizing success to build confidence and reduce anxiety."

Noah shifted from one foot to the other, kicking up sand as he did. "Hmm. That sounds interesting. How do you do it?"

Mike was happy to explain. "It's simple but powerful. Find a quiet spot where you won't be disturbed. Close your eyes and imagine yourself on the court. Visualize every detail: the feel of the ball, the movements of your teammates... Picture yourself making perfect serves, successful blocks, and winning points. Imagine how you'll feel when you're playing at your best."

Noah nodded slowly, beginning to understand. "So, it's about seeing yourself succeed before it actually happens?"

"Exactly. When you rehearse your performance in your mind, you prepare yourself for the real thing. It helps you build confidence and face challenges with a positive mindset."

Noah smiled, feeling a glimmer of hope. "That sounds like something I can try. I'll give it a shot tonight before bed."

"That's the spirit! Visualize yourself dominating on the court. You've got this. Just remember to practice the mental rehearsal regularly to see the best results."

So, before the game got started, Noah took a moment to himself. He stepped aside, closed his eyes, and began to visualize himself playing in the game. He imagined every serve, spike, and block with clarity, and for the first time all day, he felt a surge of confidence.

...

Just like Noah, you too might find yourself needing a boost before a big sports performance or any challenging situation. This chapter will talk about the Mental Rehearsal Method. By practicing mental rehearsal, you can harness your subconscious mind to envision successful outcomes. We will explore visualization exercises, discuss how resilience and emotional intelligence are connected, and dive into essential strategies to help you perform at your best. Get ready to discover how this method can elevate your mental game and lead you to success!

The Power of Mental Rehearsal

The Mental Rehearsal Method is a potent tool for creating lasting change, achieving peak performance, and gaining practical tools for consistent improvement (Steenbarger, 2018). This visualization practice has been shown to improve athletic performance by up to 24%, allowing you to train your brain to execute tasks with greater precision and confidence, even under pressure (Barnard 2014). Clearly, it is a very beneficial way to boost mental strength.

The Neuroscience of Imagination

Recent research from Stanford University has shed light on the neurological basis of mental rehearsal (Collins, 2018). Scientists found that monkeys with brain implants could improve their ability to move a cursor using arm movements simply by mentally practicing the task. This groundbreaking study demonstrates how the mental performance of a task can lead to actual learning and performance improvement.

The secret lies in motor preparation. When you vividly imagine performing an action, your brain activates many of the same neural pathways used during actual physical performance (Roychowdhury, 2022). This mental activation strengthens these pathways, making it easier for your body to execute the action in real life.

Conquering Anxiety Through Imagination

Mental rehearsal shares similarities with desensitization techniques used in psychotherapy to overcome anxiety (Raypole, 2019). By repeatedly facing threatening situations under calm, controlled emotional conditions in our minds, we can learn to respond in desired ways, free of threat.

This process works through state-dependent learning. We are best able to process and retrieve information when we return to the state in which we originally acquired that information. By vividly imagining challenging situations and then practicing effective coping strategies, we create new mental pathways that connect actual life performances with new, more positive emotional consequences.

From Imagination to Reality

Remember, effective mental rehearsal is a gateway to action. It's not just about positive thinking; it's about actively evoking the emotions associated with challenging situations and then radically shifting your state through positive coping strategies. This creates the motor preparation necessary for real-world success.

Practical Steps to Mastering Mental Rehearsal

1. Set the Scene: Find a quiet, comfortable space where you won't be disturbed.
2. Relax: Use deep breathing or progressive muscle relaxation to calm your body and mind.
3. Visualize with All Senses: Don't just see your performance; hear the sounds, feel the sensations, and even smell and taste the environment, if relevant.
4. Include Challenges: Don't just imagine perfect performances. Visualize yourself successfully overcoming obstacles and dealing with pressure.
5. Practice Regularly: Dedicate 10-15 minutes daily to mental rehearsal for the best results.
6. Combine with Physical Practice: Use mental rehearsal to complement, not replace, physical training.

It's important to point out that while we have discussed visualization as a tool to help you achieve the seven traits of mentally strong people, in this scenario, it also plays a crucial role in the Mental Rehearsal Method. Visualization is not just about imagining success; it's also about preparing your mind and body for real challenges. By visualizing your desired outcomes and rehearsing your performance mentally, you can build confidence, manage anxiety, and improve your skills.

Reflection Questions

1. Think of a challenge you're currently facing in your

athletic or personal life. How can you use the Mental Rehearsal Method to approach this challenge?
2. How can you incorporate mental rehearsal into your regular training or preparation routine? What specific times or situations will you set aside for this practice?
3. Reflect on a time when mental rehearsal didn't produce the expected results. What did you learn from that experience, and how can you adjust your approach in the future?

Summing Up

By consistently applying the Mental Rehearsal Method, you can create lasting change, achieve peak performance, and develop practical tools for consistent improvement in any area of your life. Whether you're an athlete aiming for gold, a businessperson seeking to close big deals, or simply someone striving to be their best self, mental rehearsal can help you sculpt the success you desire in your mind's eye... and then bring it to life. We've already seen how strategies like these helped the top athletes in the world overcome mental fatigue. Well, now it's time to take a deeper look at their stories to understand how exactly they did this.

Chapter 8: The Resilience Playbook: Winning Strategies from Sports and Business

"Success is where preparation and opportunity meet."
– Bobby Unser

One day, Noah and Mike sat in the living room, the glow of the television illuminating their faces as they watched the football game. The athletes on the screen moved with precision and confidence, executing plays with seemingly effortless grace.

"Wow," Noah said, shaking his head in admiration. "These athletes really know what they're doing."

Mike nodded, eyes fixed on the screen. "They make it look so easy. I know a lot about mental strength, but... I wonder what *their* daily habits are."

Noah leaned back on the couch, thoughtful. "I bet they have some pretty disciplined routines. I mean, you don't get to that level without some serious commitment."

"Well, I bet that one thing they do is mindful meditation. It helps them stay focused and calm under pressure," Mike explained. "Another habit is self-care. They make time for activities that help them relax and recharge."

Noah nodded. "Makes sense. They probably have a strict physical exercise regimen too."

"Definitely," Mike said. "But it's not just about training. They also value social connection. Having a strong support system is crucial for emotional well-being."

"And gratitude practice," Noah added, recalling a documentary he had seen. "Taking time each day to reflect on what they're thankful for keeps them grounded and positive."

Mike smiled. "Exactly. It's a whole lifestyle. They don't just train their bodies; they train their minds too."

As they continued to watch the game, Noah and Mike found themselves inspired by the athletes' dedication. They realized that achieving success, whether in sports or any other area of life, required a combination of physical and mental discipline. And with that realization, they felt motivated to incorporate some of these daily habits into their own lives.

...

Mike and Noah's story demonstrates how adopting daily strategies can lead to peak performance. Like many of us, they found inspiration in the stories of successful athletes who excel in both their mental and physical games. This chapter will explore the daily habits that drive high-performers to the top of their fields and provide practical ways for us to integrate these practices into our own lives.

Embracing the Unknown

Life, like sports, is full of uncertainties. The most successful individuals don't try to eliminate fear... they learn to navigate it. Embracing the unknown isn't about having all the answers; it's about developing the courage to face challenges directly (Chödrön, 2013). By embracing the joy of living, they let go of fear, doubt, and self-sabotage, adopting strategies that empower them to move forward with confidence and resilience.

One key strategy they use is mindful meditation, which helps ground them in the present moment and reduces anxiety about the future. Another is self-care, where they prioritize activities that bring them joy and relaxation, replenishing their energy and fostering inner peace. Physical exercise also plays a crucial role, as it boosts their physical health and releases endorphins, nature's stress relievers, and mood enhancers.

Additionally, they value social connection, making it a point to connect with loved ones daily for emotional support and a sense of belonging. Practicing gratitude is another essential habit, as it shifts their focus from what's lacking to what's present, fostering a positive outlook that's essential for bouncing back from setbacks.

By actively working on these strategies, they replace self-doubt with self-belief and transform fear into a motivating force. This approach not only helps them achieve their goals but also enhances their overall quality of life, enabling them to fully embrace the joy of living.

5 Daily Habits

Just as athletes train their bodies day in and day out, we, too, can train our minds through consistent practice. Here are five daily habits that can dramatically boost your mental resilience (VSMG, 2024):

1. Mindful Meditation

Carve out a few minutes each day to practice mindfulness. This simple act of focusing on the present moment can calm your mind, reduce stress, and enhance your ability to cope with challenges. Find a quiet spot, sit comfortably, and bring your attention to your breath or surroundings. When your mind wanders (and it will), gently guide it back to the present. You can find more information about mindfulness in our earlier chapter 5.

2. Self-Care

Prioritize activities that bring you joy and relaxation. Whether it's reading a book, taking a leisurely walk in nature, or indulging in a hobby, self-care replenishes your energy reserves and fosters inner peace. Remember, you can't pour from an empty cup.

3. Physical Exercise

The mind-body connection is powerful. Regular exercise not only boosts your physical health but also releases endorphins – nature's stress relievers and mood enhancers.

Aim for at least 30 minutes of moderate exercise daily, choosing activities you genuinely enjoy.

4. Social Connection

Even the toughest athletes rely on a support system. Make it a point to connect with loved ones daily. A quick call, a shared meal, or even a thoughtful text can provide the emotional support and sense of belonging crucial for resilience.

5. Gratitude Practice

Take a moment each day to reflect on what you're thankful for. This simple act can shift your focus from what's lacking to what's present, fostering a positive outlook that's essential for bouncing back from setbacks.

Strategies from the World's Best

The path to athletic excellence extends beyond physical prowess. It involves a rigorous mental regimen that reprograms the subconscious mind, overcomes mental barriers, and unlocks its full potential. This case study explores how successful athletes and high-performers harness the power of mindful meditation, self-care, physical exercise, social connection, and gratitude practice to achieve peak performance.

Mindful Meditation: Kobe Bryant

Kobe Bryant, one of the greatest basketball players of all time, was a strong advocate of mindful meditation. He believed it played a critical role in his success by enhancing his focus and composure under pressure (Ballesteros, 2018). Bryant practiced mindfulness daily, often beginning his day with meditation sessions to clear his mind and set a positive tone. This habit allowed him to maintain unparalleled mental clarity and perform at his best during high-stakes moments on the court.

Self-Care: Roger Federer

Tennis legend Roger Federer attributes much of his longevity and success to his commitment to self-care. He prioritizes activities that bring him joy and relaxation, such as spending time with family, indulging in hobbies like playing the piano, and ensuring adequate rest and recovery (Badger, 2023). Federer's dedication to self-care has helped him sustain a high level of performance over two decades, reducing the risk of burnout and injuries.

Physical Exercise: Michael Phelps

Michael Phelps, the most decorated Olympian of all time, exemplifies the power of a rigorous physical exercise routine. Phelps' training regimen is famously intense, involving swimming for up to six hours a day, six days a week (Mikkelsen, 2023). Beyond swimming, he incorporates weightlifting, stretching, and other physical activities to enhance his strength, flexibility, and endurance. This unwavering commitment to physical exercise has enabled Phelps to achieve extraordinary feats in the pool.

Social Connection: Serena Williams

Serena Williams, who we've talked about a bunch in this book, values social connection as a cornerstone of her mental resilience. She maintains close relationships with her family, especially her sister Venus, who is also a professional tennis player. Serena often speaks about the emotional support she receives from her loved ones, which helps her stay grounded and motivated (Wilson, 2015). The strength of these connections has been crucial in her ability to overcome challenges and setbacks throughout her career.

Gratitude Practice: Tom Brady

Tom Brady, a seven-time Super Bowl champion that we have mentioned earlier, incorporates gratitude practice into his daily routine. Brady frequently reflects on what he is thankful for, whether it's his health, family, teammates, or the opportunities he has had in his career. Even when faced with a huge loss in the 2022 playoffs, he remained thankful over anything else (Wegner 2022). By focusing on gratitude, Brady maintains a positive outlook and stays motivated to continue performing at an elite level. This practice has been instrumental in his mental toughness and ability to persevere through the demands of professional football.

Reflection Questions

1. What are your current daily habits? How do they align with the habits discussed in this chapter?
2. How do these stories motivate you to push beyond your current limits?
3. Which of the daily habits discussed in this chapter do you plan to incorporate into your routine first?
4. What long-term goals do you have, and how will these habits help you achieve them?

Summing Up

As you work on building your mental resilience, remember that the goal is not just to endure life's challenges, but to find joy in the journey. Embrace each day as an opportunity for growth, connection, and discovery.

The success of athletes like Kobe Bryant, Roger Federer, Michael Phelps, Serena Williams, and Tom Brady highlights the importance of a holistic approach to mental training. By incorporating these strategies and habits into your daily life, you're not just preparing for adversity, you're cultivating a mindset that allows you to thrive in any circumstance. Remember, mental resilience isn't about eliminating fear or uncertainty. It's about developing the tools to navigate life's twists and turns with grace, courage, and even excitement for what lies ahead.

So, are you ready to unlock your full potential and embrace life's beautiful unpredictability? The next chapter will discuss daily exercises to activate mental strength and perform at your best.

Chapter 9: 11 Daily Exercises for Peak Performance

"I always felt that my greatest asset was not my physical ability, it was my mental ability."
- Bruce Jenner

One weekend, Noah and Mike had decided to spend their Saturday exploring a new trail just outside town. The crisp autumn air was filled with the scent of pine and the crunch of leaves underfoot as they jogged along the winding path. The trail was more challenging than Noah had anticipated, with steep inclines and uneven terrain that tested their endurance.

As they reached a clearing with a stunning view of the valley below, they took a break to catch their breath. Noah sat on a large rock, admiring the scenery, while Mike leaned against a tree, stretching his legs.

"Wow, this trail is no joke," Noah said, wiping sweat from his brow. "Those pro runners make it look so easy on TV. I wonder what they do to stay at the top of their game."

Mike took a deep breath of the fresh mountain air and smiled. "You know, it's not just about physical training for them. They have some powerful daily habits that help them achieve peak performance."

Noah raised his eyebrows in curiosity. "What kind of habits are we talking about?"

Mike sat down on the ground beside him and began to explain. "Well, one key habit is mindfulness. Take someone like trail runner Courtney Dauwalter. She's known for her mindfulness practice, where she focuses on being present in the moment, whether she's running through challenging terrain or during recovery. It helps her stay calm and focused even in intense situations. (Pryor 2023)."

Noah nodded, thinking about the peaceful forest around them. "That makes sense. It's about being in the moment, just like we are right now."

Mike continued, "Another important habit is self-compassion. For instance, ultramarathoner Scott Jurek practices self-compassion by acknowledging that every race won't be perfect. He learns from his experiences rather than beating himself up (Finn 2017)."

"That sounds really useful," Noah said. "What about stepping out of your comfort zone?"

Mike grinned. "Ah, yes. Look at the story of marathon runner Des Linden. She stepped out of her comfort zone by embracing extreme weather conditions during the Boston Marathon. She believes that growth happens when we push beyond what's comfortable (Ford, 2018)."

Noah glanced around at the rugged trail they had just run. "I guess we're doing that right now!"

Mike laughed. "Exactly. Another crucial habit is processing your feelings. Take Eliud Kipchoge, the world record-holding marathoner. He processes his feelings through techniques like journaling and reflection, helping him manage the highs and lows of his career (Kipchoge, 2019)."

"That's interesting," Noah said. "And how do they keep a balanced perspective?"

Mike began walking again, and Noah followed. "Athletes like Meb Keflezighi use techniques to maintain perspective on their challenges. Meb reflects on the bigger picture and avoids letting setbacks define him. He uses questions like, 'Is this challenge permanent? Is it all-encompassing? Is it my fault?' to stay balanced (Keflezighi n.d.)."

They continued down the trail, feeling invigorated from the exercise. "What about social connections?" Noah asked as they approached a scenic overlook.

"Strong support systems are crucial for athletes," Mike said. "Take Olympic swimmer Katie Ledecky, who has a close-knit team of coaches, family, and friends (Maese, 2021). They help her stay motivated and grounded."

"That makes sense," Noah said, catching his breath. "And what about goal-setting?"

Mike pointed to the trail they had just navigated. "Athletes like Eliud Kipchoge set clear, actionable goals for themselves. Kipchoge's goals are specific, measurable, and time-bound, like aiming to break records and improve his techniques (Mwangi, 2023)."

Noah took a deep breath, appreciating the view. "I see. And how do they practice gratitude?"

Mike smiled. "Athletes like Serena Williams integrate gratitude into their daily routines. She takes time each day to reflect on what she's thankful for, which helps her stay positive and focused (Heo, 2023)."

"And mental stamina?" Noah asked as they resumed their run.

"Mentally strong athletes practice techniques like the Pomodoro Technique to build endurance," Mike explained. "They work intensely in short bursts, with breaks in between, gradually increasing their stamina."

Noah was curious. "And brain-boosting activities?"

Mike chuckled. "Athletes often engage in brain-boosting activities like solving puzzles or learning new skills. For example, some runners use strategy games to sharpen their decision-making skills."

As they finished their run and headed back to the parking lot, Noah reflected on what Mike had shared.

"Mike, I never realized how much goes into an athlete's routine beyond just training their bodies," Noah said, feeling inspired.

Mike clapped him on the back. "That's right. These daily habits can help anyone build mental strength and reach their full potential."

...

Mike and Noah now know all about strategies to build mental strength. This chapter presents a powerful playbook of 11 daily exercises designed to activate your mental muscles and help you perform at your best. By incorporating these practices into your routine, you'll build resilience, sharpen focus, and unlock your full potential.

1. Practice Mindfulness

Imagine your mind as a busy intersection. Mindfulness is your ability to direct traffic, focusing on what matters most right now. Research shows that regular mindfulness practice can reduce stress, improve emotional regulation, and enhance overall well-being (Creswell, 2019).

Chapter 5 provides excellent examples of how to implement mindfulness into your daily routine. Here is another idea for you to try: Set aside 5-10 minutes daily for a simple breathing meditation. Focus on the sensation of your breath entering and leaving your body. When your mind wanders (and it will), gently redirect your attention back to your breath without judgment.

2. Embrace Self-Compassion

Self-compassion isn't self-indulgence; it's a vital skill for mental toughness. Studies reveal that individuals who practice self-compassion are more resilient in the face of setbacks and better equipped to bounce back from failure (Chen, 2018).

Chapter 4 explored self-compassion in-depth, but here is another helpful exercise: When you make a mistake or face a challenge, pause and ask yourself, "How would I speak to a good friend in this situation?" Then, offer yourself that same kindness and understanding.

3. Step Out of Your Comfort Zone

Your comfort zone might feel safe, but it's also where

growth stagnates. Regularly pushing your boundaries builds confidence and adaptability (Paige, 2014).

We touched upon this in our Chapter 4 discussion about growth mindset. Here is a challenge to build from that: Each week, do one thing that makes you slightly uncomfortable. It could be striking up a conversation with a stranger, trying a new hobby, or tackling a task you've been avoiding.

4. Acknowledge and Process Your Feelings

Suppressing emotions doesn't make them disappear; it often amplifies them. Learning to recognize and process your feelings is crucial for mental strength.

Try this: Keep a daily emotion log. An emotion log is a simple yet effective tool for tracking and reflecting on your emotional experiences (Wright, 2023). It helps you identify patterns in your emotions, understand what triggers them, and develop strategies for managing them. The process involves recording your emotions daily, along with the events or situations that prompted them. Over time, you'll develop greater emotional awareness and insight.

Example Emotion Log	
After each significant sports activity, write down three emotions you felt. For each emotion, include the following details:	
Emotion: The specific feeling you experienced (e.g., frustration, excitement, nervousness). **Trigger:** The event or situation that caused this emotion (e.g., a missed shot during practice, a successful game, a disagreement with a coach). **Intensity:** Rate the strength of the emotion on a scale from 1 to 10 (1 being mild and 10 being intense). **Reflection:** Briefly reflect on how you dealt with the emotion and what you could do differently next time.	**Emotion:** Frustration **Trigger:** Missed a crucial goal in the match **Intensity:** 8/10 **Reflection:** I felt frustrated about missing the goal. Next time, I will focus on my technique during practice and remind myself that one mistake doesn't define my performance.

5. Keep a Balanced Perspective

How you perceive challenges directly impacts your ability to overcome them. Developing a balanced perspective allows you to see opportunities where others might only see obstacles.

In sports and everyday life, it's easy to get caught up in the intensity of a situation, allowing a single setback to feel overwhelming. The "3 Ps" technique—Permanent, Pervasive, and Personal—is a cognitive reframing tool that helps you break down and manage your thoughts during challenging times (Holstee, 2024). This technique encourages you to question your automatic negative thoughts and view problems with a clearer, more balanced perspective (Seligman, 2006).

Example "3 Ps"	
Permanent "Is This Issue Going to Last Forever?"	Example: You miss a crucial shot in a basketball game. You might think, "I'm never going to be good at this." However, this mistake does not define your entire ability as a player.
Pervasive "Is This Issue Affecting All Areas of My Life?"	Example: After a poor performance in a tennis match, you might think, "I'm bad at sports, and I'm failing at everything." Understand that a single setback in sports does not reflect your overall abilities or self-worth.
Personal "Is This My Fault?"	Example: If your team loses a match, you might think, "It's all my fault; I let everyone down." Recognize that losses are often a result of multiple factors, not just your own actions.

6. Practice Self-Care: Fueling Your Mental Engine

Your brain is an organ, and like any organ, it needs proper care to function optimally. Self-care isn't selfish; it's essential for mental strength and overall well-being. This was touched upon a little in Chapter 4, but it's important to restate.

Daily habits: Prioritize 7-9 hours of sleep, eat a balanced

diet rich in brain-boosting foods (like omega-3 fatty acids and antioxidants), and aim for at least 30 minutes of moderate exercise daily (Morin, 2020).

7. Build Meaningful Connections: The Power of Social Support

Humans are social creatures, and strong relationships are a cornerstone of mental resilience. Research consistently shows that people with robust social networks are better equipped to handle stress and adversity (Reid, n.d).

Challenge: Reach out to one person in your network each day, even if it's just a quick message or call. Nurture your relationships consistently.

8. Set Clear Goals and Pursue Them Persistently: The Roadmap to Success

Goals provide direction and purpose, essential elements of mental toughness. But it's not enough to simply set goals; you must actively work toward them.

Try this: Use the SMART framework (Specific, Measurable, Achievable, Relevant, Time-bound) to set one short-term and one long-term goal. Break them down into smaller, actionable steps and track your progress daily (Boogaard, 2023).

Example S.M.A.R.T Goals			
Acronym	Definition	What it Means	Example
S	Specific: Define Your Goal Clearly	A specific goal is clear and detailed, answering the "who," "what," "where," "when," and "why" of your objective.	Instead of saying, "I want to improve my tennis skills," say, "I want to increase my first serve accuracy to 75% in practice sessions."
M	Measurable: Track Your Progress	A measurable goal includes criteria for tracking your progress and determining success.	"I will measure my serve accuracy each week by recording the number of successful serves out of 20 attempts."
A	Achievable: Set Realistic Targets	An achievable goal is realistic and attainable given your current resources and constraints.	"I will dedicate 30 minutes of each practice session specifically to working on my serve."
R	Relevant: Align Goals with Your Bigger Objectives	A relevant goal aligns with your long-term aspirations and overall objectives.	"Improving my serve accuracy will help me perform better in matches and contribute to my goal of becoming a competitive tennis player."
T	Time-bound: Set a Deadline	A time-bound goal has a clear deadline for completion.	"I will achieve my goal by the end of the three-month training period."

9. Develop Gratitude: Shifting Your Focus

Gratitude isn't just a feel-good practice; it's a powerful tool for building mental strength. Regular gratitude exercises have been shown to increase happiness, reduce depression, and improve overall life satisfaction (Mosunic, n.d.).

Daily habit: Before bed each night, write down three

things you're grateful for. They can be big or small but try to be specific and vary your entries day to day.

10. Enhance Mental Stamina: Training Your Brain Like a Muscle

Just as you'd train for a marathon, you can build your mental endurance over time. This allows you to stay focused and perform under pressure for longer periods.

Exercise: Practice the "Pomodoro Technique." This is a time-management method that breaks work into short, focused intervals, known as Pomodoros, followed by brief breaks (Boogaard, 2023). Developed by Francesco Cirillo in the late 1980s, the technique is named after the Italian word for "tomato," inspired by the tomato-shaped kitchen timer Cirillo used during university. The basic structure of the Pomodoro Technique goes as follows:

1. Work for 25 minutes: Concentrate on a specific task without interruptions.
2. Take a 5-minute break: Rest and recharge.
3. Repeat: Complete three more Pomodoros, then take a longer break of 15-30 minutes.

Believe it or not, the Pomodoro Technique helps you set and achieve short-term goals, which is vital for long-term sports success. For example, if you're training for a marathon, use the Pomodoro Technique to structure your running sessions. You can run for 25 minutes at a challenging pace, then take a 5-minute break to hydrate and stretch.

Repeat this process for a total of four Pomodoros. During each Pomodoro, concentrate on your running form or specific aspects of your training, such as pacing or breathing techniques.

Example Pomodoro Technique	
25 minutes	Run at a steady pace focusing on form.
5-minute break	Stretch and rehydrate.
25 minutes	Run intervals or perform speed drills.
5-minute break	Light stretching and deep breathing.
25 minutes	Endurance run or practice long-distance strategy.
5-minute break	Reflect on performance and set goals for the next session.

This approach helps build mental stamina, manage time efficiently, and maintain high performance under pressure.

11. Engage in Brain-Boosting Activities: Cognitive Cross-Training

Your brain thrives on novelty and challenge. Engaging in diverse mental activities helps build new neural connections and maintain cognitive flexibility (Paffett, 2023).

Daily challenge: Incorporate one brain-boosting activity into your routine each day. This could be solving a puzzle, learning a few words in a new language, or practicing a musical instrument for 15 minutes.

Reflection Questions

1. How can you incorporate mindfulness into your daily routine to enhance focus and reduce stress?
2. When facing setbacks, how can you practice self-compassion to maintain resilience?
3. What is one new challenge you can undertake to push beyond your comfort zone and encourage personal growth?
4. How can you use journaling or reflection to better understand and manage your emotions?
5. What are some strategies you can use to maintain a balanced perspective when dealing with obstacles or challenges?
6. What steps can you take to improve your self-care routine for better mental and physical health?
7. How can you strengthen your social connections to provide support and encouragement in your personal and professional life?
8. What are some specific short-term and long-term goals you can set using the SMART framework?
9. How can you start a daily gratitude practice to foster a more positive outlook?
10. What techniques can you use to improve your mental stamina and productivity in your daily tasks?
11. What new brain-boosting activities can you try to challenge yourself and stimulate cognitive growth?

Summing Up

Hold onto these 11 powerful strategies for developing mental strength and achieving peak performance. From practicing mindfulness and embracing self-compassion to stepping out of your comfort zone and setting clear goals, these daily exercises offer practical ways to build resilience, sharpen your focus, and unlock your full potential.

But remember, building mental strength is a journey, not a destination. Just as a fire needs time to grow from a single spark into a blazing flame, so too do these practices require consistent effort and patience. Consistency is key; small, regular efforts will accumulate over time, leading to significant personal growth and transformation.

Just as humanity has been captivated by the elemental force of fire throughout history, you can harness the metaphor of the fire to understand and embrace your mental strength journey. Now, it's time to take the idea of that "fire" to the next chapter, where we will discuss reflective practices in the form of a fireside reflection.

Chapter 10: Fireside Reflection

"Each of us has a fire in our hearts for something. It's our goal in life to find it and keep it lit."
– Mary Lou Retton

As the sun dipped below the horizon, casting long shadows across the landscape, Noah and Mike sat beside the crackling campfire. The warmth of the flames contrasted with the crisp evening air, and the flickering light danced across their faces. They had spent the day hiking through the rugged terrain of the forest, and now, as darkness enveloped them, the fire became their sanctuary, a place for conversation and reflection.

We know that Noah had been grappling with the weight of his own mental struggles for months. He had wrestled with self-doubt and insecurity, feeling as though he was constantly treading water but never really making progress.

But tonight, things were different. He had recently learned about the principles of mental strength from Mike, who had become his mentor and guide.

As they settled into their camping chairs, Noah stared at the flames, lost in thought. Mike noticed his contemplative silence and decided it was time to share what he had learned about mental strength.

"Hey, Noah," Mike began, breaking the silence, "You've come such a long way with your mental strength. I want to share one thing with you that might help."

Noah looked up, his curiosity piqued. "What do you have in mind?"

Mike took a deep breath, letting the warmth of the fire envelop him. "I want to talk to you about the concept of fireside reflection and how it can be a powerful tool for building mental strength. It's something that has been used throughout history and can be incredibly effective if you practice it right."

Noah leaned in, eager to hear more. "How does it work?"

Mike gestured toward the fire. "You see, just sitting here and gazing at the flames can bring about a state of relaxation and contemplation. It's a form of mindfulness that allows you to quiet your mind and focus on the present moment. When I was struggling, I found that simply sitting by a fire like this helped me calm my nerves and reflect on my challenges."

He watched as Noah's eyes followed the flames, the rhythmic movement of the fire capturing his attention. "The idea is to let the fire's natural rhythm guide you into a meditative state," Mike continued. "It's not about thinking hard or trying to solve everything at once. It's about creating a space where your thoughts can flow freely, helping you gain insights and clarity."

Noah nodded, beginning to understand. "So it's like a form of meditation?"

"Exactly," Mike said. "It's a form of mindfulness that helps you stay present and reduce stress. When I was training, I used this technique to manage my anxiety and stay focused. I'd spend a few minutes every evening just watching the flames, and it made a big difference."

As Mike spoke, Noah tried to immerse himself in the simplicity of the fire's light. The flames flickered and swayed, and he let his thoughts drift away from the pressures of competition. The soothing effect of the fire began to wash over him, easing the tension that had been building up.

"Another method that helped me was visualization," Mike said, breaking Noah's reverie. "While you're focusing on the fire, you can also visualize your goals and imagine yourself achieving them. This practice helps reinforce your commitment and motivates you to keep pushing forward."

Noah took a deep breath and closed his eyes, visualizing himself performing at his best. He imagined the thrill of victory, the satisfaction of achieving his goals, and the pride of overcoming obstacles. The exercise was both calming and inspiring.

"Visualization is a powerful tool," Mike said softly. "It's about creating a mental image of your success and using that to drive your actions. When you face challenges, remembering those images can help you stay motivated and focused."

Noah opened his eyes and looked at Mike with newfound resolve. "I can see how this could help. I've been so caught up in my doubts and fears that I forgot to think about what I'm working toward."

Mike smiled, pleased to see Noah's shift in perspective. "Another important thing is self-reflection. While you're here, take some time to think about your experiences, both the successes and the failures. Reflect on what you've learned and how you can use those lessons to improve."

Noah took this advice to heart, allowing himself to reflect on his recent challenges and victories. The calm of the fire provided the perfect backdrop for this introspection. He thought about the moments when he had succeeded and those when he had fallen short, using the time to understand his emotions and plan his next steps.

"Self-reflection helped me a lot when I was feeling lost," Mike said, watching as Noah thoughtfully gazed at the flames. "It's a way to understand your journey and figure out where you want to go next. It's not always easy, but it's a valuable part of building mental strength."

Noah nodded, feeling a sense of clarity. "I think I understand now. It's about finding calm, focusing on your goals, and learning from your experiences."

"Exactly," Mike agreed. "And remember, it's a process. You don't have to have all the answers right away. Just keep practicing these techniques, and over time, you'll build the mental strength you need."

As the fire crackled and popped, Noah felt a renewed sense of hope. The simple act of sitting by the fire, combined with Mike's guidance, had helped him see a path forward. He was ready to embrace the practices of relaxation, visualization, and self-reflection that Mike had shared.

...

Just like Noah and Mike used the fireside to explore techniques for mental strength, you, too, can harness these practices to enhance your resilience and focus. In this chapter, we will learn about the art of fire gazing, a timeless practice that encourages relaxation and introspection. You will learn how to use this simple yet powerful technique to calm your mind and foster a state of mindfulness.

An Ancient Man's Reflective Practice

Throughout history, fire has held a mesmerizing allure for humanity. Whether around a campfire, hearth, or candle, the act of gazing into flames transcends mere physical warmth. For men seeking mental strength, this creative space of fireside reflection can be a valuable resource for problem-solving and self-reflection (Wynn, 2012).

Connection to Ancient Wisdom

In ancient times, the fire of the hearth was central to domestic life. The hearth was not just a source of heat but also a place where families gathered to share stories and discuss important matters. For example, in Homer's The Iliad, the hearth of the palace served as a place for heroes and leaders to plan their strategies and reflect on their actions. The communal fire provided a setting for dialogue and decision-making that shaped the course of the epic conflict.

Similarly, during the Middle Ages, the hearth in monasteries and abbeys was often the site of contemplation and intellectual discussion. Monks would gather around the fire to engage in theological debates and philosophical reflections.

For instance, Thomas Aquinas, one of the most influential medieval theologians, likely engaged in deep thought and scholarly discussion by the fireside in his quest to reconcile faith with reason (Murphy, 2022).

In more recent history, the campfire has been a symbol of both adventure and introspection. American frontiersmen and explorers, such as Lewis and Clark, used the campfire on their expeditions to reflect on their journey, strategize for future endeavors, and bond with their companions (Ronda, 1984). The simple act of sitting around a campfire provided a moment of pause amid their challenging expeditions, offering a mental space to process their experiences and plan their next steps.

Clearly, fire has an enduring allure, a source of comfort and insight, across different historical periods. This shows us that it is a tool for mental fortitude and personal growth.

The Science Behind Reflection

Recent research has shed light on the neurological impacts of fire gazing. A study on the effects of fire gazing on brain activity and relaxation found that watching flames can induce a state of calm focus, increasing alpha brain waves associated with relaxation and meditative states (Lynn, 2014). When we gaze into a fire, our brains experience changes that promote relaxation and mental clarity. This effect is linked to the increase in alpha brain waves. Alpha brain waves, which oscillate between 8 and 12 Hz, are commonly associated with states of relaxation, peacefulness, and reduced stress (Cherry, 2023). These waves are prevalent during moments of calm wakefulness, such as when you're daydreaming or meditating.

This practice goes beyond simple stress reduction. Psychological studies, like Laura King's work, highlight how intentional reflection can boost emotional intelligence, self-awareness, and overall well-being (King, 2001). Her research shows that this practice is a cornerstone of positive psychology, which focuses on enhancing life satisfaction and emotional resilience.

Modern science has shown us that observing fire activates relaxation-related brain regions. The flickering flames engage the brain in a manner like mindfulness practices. The consistent, gentle motion of the fire provides a visual focus that helps calm the mind, like how focusing on a meditative object can help achieve a state of mental ease.

Modern Adaptation

By engaging in fireside reflection, modern men can tap into these primal instincts and archetypal energies. The flickering flames provide a link to our collective past, allowing us to access deeper levels of consciousness and wisdom (Very Big Brain, 2023).

While gathering around an actual fire may only sometimes be practical in today's world, the essence of fireside reflection can be adapted to modern life. In the next section, we will explore how we can apply this to our daily lives and in sports.

How to Practice Fireside Reflection and the Benefits

Fireside reflection offers athletes a unique opportunity for relaxation, creative thinking, and mindfulness, all of which are essential for developing mental strength and enhancing performance. Here's how to practice fireside reflection and how these practices can benefit athletes in their sports careers.

Relaxation and Contemplation

We already discussed how early humans used the campfire for physical needs, social interaction, and reflection, drawing on the fire's soothing qualities to calm their minds and foster thoughtful discussions.

For modern athletes, fireside reflection can be an effective way to achieve relaxation and introspection. The rhythmic dance of flames has a mesmerizing effect that encourages a state of calm. When athletes take time to sit by a fire, they enter a space where their thoughts can flow freely, helping them to process their experiences, set goals, and evaluate their performance. The warmth and glow of the fire create a serene environment that supports mental relaxation and emotional balance.

Imagine a soccer player who has just finished a challenging match. By sitting by a fire and allowing their mind to settle, the player can reflect on their performance, understand what went well, and identify areas for improvement. This practice helps them to process their thoughts in a calm setting, leading to clearer insights and a more focused approach for future games (Very Big Brain, 2023).

Creative Thinking and Inspiration

As we know, ancient philosophers and storytellers would gather around the fire to share ideas and inspire one another. The fire's flickering light created an atmosphere conducive to imaginative thinking and problem-solving.

Likewise, sitting by a fire can spark creativity and original thinking for athletes. The flames' gentle and dynamic movement helps the mind wander beyond everyday concerns, allowing new ideas and strategies to emerge. For instance, a basketball coach might use the fireside setting to brainstorm new plays or reflect on innovative training techniques.

Consider a tennis player facing a plateau in their performance. By engaging in fireside reflection, they can use the calming influence of the flames to explore new training methods, reevaluate their techniques, or come up with creative solutions to overcome challenges. This creative space helps athletes break free from conventional thinking and discover new ways to enhance their skills (Very Big Brain, 2023).

Mindfulness and Stress Reduction:

We have seen that focusing on the fire's gentle, unending movement helps individuals achieve a meditative state where they can find peace and tranquility away from daily stressors.

Fire gazing is a form of mindfulness practice that encourages athletes to be fully present in the moment. As athletes focus on the flames, they can let go of their worries and stressors, creating a mental space where they can recharge and refocus. This practice can be particularly beneficial during high-pressure times, such as before an important competition.

Before a big game, a football player might take time to sit by a fire to practice mindfulness. This quiet moment of focusing on the fire helps the player manage pre-game anxiety and maintain a calm, centered mindset. The simplicity of the fire provides a welcome break from the complexities and pressures of competition, allowing the player to approach the game with a clear and composed mental state.

Candle Meditation and Cognitive Enhancement:

Candle-gazing meditation, a practice that involves focusing on a candle flame, has been used throughout history for its meditative and cognitive benefits. Concentrating on the flame promotes mental clarity and emotional stability (Mayer, 2022). By simply gazing at the steady light of a candle, practitioners can harness the power of this simple yet profound practice to enhance their mental and emotional well-being.

Recent research highlights several cognitive and emotional benefits of candle meditation, which are particularly relevant for athletes looking to improve their mental performance and emotional resilience.

One of the primary benefits of candle meditation is that it encourages introspection and mental clarity. The practice offers a quiet space for self-reflection, allowing individuals to explore their thoughts and emotions more deeply. This mental clarity can help athletes evaluate their performance, set new goals, and develop strategies for improvement (Mayer, 2022).

For athletes, self-reflection is the key to growth and development. Candle meditation provides a reflective space where athletes can assess their progress, contemplate their challenges, and plan their next steps. This practice supports personal growth and helps athletes stay aligned with their long-term objectives.

A tennis player might use candle meditation after a match to reflect on their performance. This time allows them to think about what worked well and what could be improved, leading to more effective training and future success (Mayer, 2022).

	How to Practice Candle Meditation
1. Find a Quiet Space	Choose a quiet and comfortable place where you can sit undisturbed. Set up a candle in front of you at eye level, so you can gaze at the flame comfortably.
2. Set Your Intentions	Before you begin, take a moment to set your intentions for the practice. Decide what you want to achieve, whether it's reducing stress, improving focus, or gaining insight.
3. Gaze at the Flame	Light the candle and focus your attention on the flame. Observe the way it flickers and moves. Try to keep your mind centered on the candle's light and let go of other thoughts.
4. Breathe Deeply	Take slow, deep breaths as you focus on the flame. This helps to relax your body and mind, enhancing the meditative experience.
5. Reflect and Absorb	Allow yourself to enter a state of mindfulness. Let the flame's gentle motion guide you into a state of calm reflection. After the practice, take some time to absorb any insights or thoughts that came up.

Athletes can integrate candle meditation into their routines to leverage its benefits for performance enhancement. First, they can start a Pre-Competition ritual. Imagine using candle meditation as a pre-competition ritual to calm your mind and focus on your performance goals. Of course, they can also conduct a Post-Training Reflection. Implement candle meditation after training sessions to reflect on your progress, identify areas for improvement, and mentally prepare for future challenges. And, we can't forget Daily Mindfulness Practice. Athletes can incorporate candle meditation into their daily routines to maintain mental clarity, manage stress, and foster emotional balance.

By incorporating candle meditation into your regular routine, you can develop a stronger, more resilient mindset that will benefit you both on and off the field.

Reflection Questions

1. How might regular fireside reflection enhance your problem-solving abilities in daily life?
2. In what ways could this practice help you connect with your inner wisdom?
3. How could you adapt fireside reflection to fit into your current lifestyle?
4. What insights or realizations have you had during moments of quiet contemplation?

Summing Up

In this chapter, we learned about the ancient practice of fireside reflection and its relevance to modern life. Historically, sitting around a fire was more than a way to stay warm; it was a time for deep conversations, storytelling, and personal introspection. In a world that moves quickly, taking time for personal reflection can offer deep mental and emotional benefits.

We also learned that this practice is highly relevant to athletes today. Just as fireside gatherings helped people reflect on their experiences, athletes can use personal reflection to analyze their performances and prepare for future challenges. By setting aside time for thoughtful reflection, athletes can strengthen their mental resilience and improve their game. Will you accept the invitation to explore the transformative power of fireside reflection?

Conclusion

"Obstacles don't have to stop you. If you run into a wall, don't turn around and give up. Figure out how to climb it, go through it, or work around it."
-Michael Jordan

As we come to the end of our journey together, let's reflect on what we've learned and how you can use these lessons to transform your own life. We've explored what it truly means to develop mental strength. We've discovered that mental strength is about more than just being resilient. It's about emotional intelligence, self-discipline, persistence, and the ability to endure through challenges. The good news is that these qualities aren't reserved for a select few... they can be developed by anyone willing to put in the effort.

To illustrate this, let's think back to Michael Jordan's story. Remember how he was cut from the varsity basketball team as a sophomore because he was considered too short? For many, this might have been seen as the end of the road. But Jordan saw it as a challenge. Instead of giving up, he used that disappointment as motivation to work harder. His journey from being cut from the team to becoming one of the greatest basketball players of all time shows us that mental toughness is not just about natural talent but about how we face our obstacles and stay focused on our goals.

Throughout this book, we've covered strategies for building mental strength. We've talked about understanding your emotions and those of others, staying disciplined, bouncing back from failures, and enduring tough times.

We also addressed common struggles you might face, such as self-doubt, overcoming obstacles, and reaching for your goals. These are challenges everyone experiences, whether in sports, work, or personal growth.

Now it's time to take what you've learned and put it into action. Here are some practical steps you can take:

First, see setbacks as opportunities. Like Michael Jordan, view challenges as chances for growth. When you face a setback, reflect on what you can learn from it and how it can strengthen you.

Next, keep practicing the mental strength exercises from this book. Make these exercises part of your daily routine to build and maintain your mental toughness.

Set clear, achievable goals for yourself. Break them into smaller steps, and celebrate your progress along the way.

Work on developing your emotional intelligence. Practice understanding and managing your emotions, and work on being empathetic and supportive in your relationships with others.

Adopt a growth mindset. Embrace new challenges as opportunities to learn and grow.

Stay committed to your journey. Just as Jordan dedicated himself to his training, stay focused on your goals and keep pushing through adversity.

Build a support network. Surround yourself with people who encourage and support you in your growth.

As you move forward, remember that the path to mental strength is a lifelong journey. The lessons from this book are not just for this moment, but for every challenge you will face. The stories of all the athletes in this book show us that success is not just about natural ability, but about how we respond to challenges and stay committed to our goals.

Are you ready to take these lessons and apply them to your own life? To tap into your inner star-athlete and face your challenges with determination and strength? Your journey toward mental mastery begins now. I believe in your potential, and I'm excited to see where your path will take you.

References

AQR International. (n.d.). Nature vs nurture: What this means for mental toughness. https://aqrinternational.co.uk/nature-vs-nurture-what-this-means-for-mental-toughness

Ballesteros, C. (2018, August 8). Mindfulness: The secret weapon of Michael Jordan and Kobe Bryant. MARCA. Adapted by Panos Kostopoulos. https://www.marca.com/en/more-sports/2018/08/08/5b6b082f22601d291e8b45b9.html

Barnard, D. (2019, April 4). The power of mindset on sports performance. SportsMD. https://www.sportsmd.com/2019/04/04/the-power-of-mindset-on-sports-performance/

Believe Perform. (n.d.). Mental toughness: Nature vs nurture. https://members.believeperform.com/mental-toughness-nature-vs-nurture/

Boogaard, K. (2023, December 17). The Pomodoro Technique: Boosting productivity with time management. Lark Suite. https://www.larksuite.com/en_us/topics/productivity-glossary/the-pomodoro-technique

Boogaard, K. (2023, January 18). The Pomodoro Technique really works, says this productivity-hack skeptic. The Muse. https://www.themuse.com/advice/take-it-from-someone-who-hates-productivity-hacksthe-pomodoro-technique-actually-works

Brandman, M. (2020-2022). Serena Williams. National Women's History Museum. https://www.womenshistory.org/education-resources/biographies/serena-williams

Britannica, T. Editors of Encyclopaedia. (2023, July 27). Pelé. Encyclopaedia Britannica. https://www.britannica.com/biography/Pele-Brazilian-athlete

Brown, D. L. (2018, June 16). 'Shoot them for what?' How Muhammad Ali won his greatest fight. The Washington Post. https://www.washingtonpost.com/news/retropolis/wp/2018/06/15/shoot-them-for-what-how-muhammad-ali-won-his-greatest-fight/

Calm. (n.d.). Mental strength. https://www.calm.com/blog/mental-strength

CD Lynn. (2014). Hearth and campfire influences on arterial blood pressure: Defraying the costs of the social brain through fireside relaxation. Evolutionary Psychology, 12(5), 983-1003. https://epjournal.net/3397

Chen, S. (2018, September). Give yourself a break: The power of self-compassion. Harvard Business Review. https://hbr.org/2018/09/give-yourself-a-break-the-power-of-self-compassion

Cherry, K. (2023, September 12). What are alpha brain waves? Increasing alpha waves may reduce depression. Verywell Mind. https://www.verywellmind.com/what-are-alpha-brain-waves-2794851

Cherry, K. (2024, May 09). How to boost your self-awareness. Verywell Mind. https://www.verywellmind.com/what-is-self-awareness-2795023

Chödrön, P. (2013). Living beautifully: With uncertainty and change. Shambhala.

Clear, J. (2018). Atomic habits: An easy & proven way to build good habits & break bad ones. Penguin Random House.

Collins, N. (2018, February 15). Mental rehearsal prepares our minds for real-world action, Stanford researchers find. Stanford News. https://news.stanford.edu/stories/2018/02/mental-rehearsal-might-prepare-minds-action

Cote, C. (2022, March 10). Growth mindset vs. fixed mindset: What's the difference? Harvard Business School Online. https://online.hbs.edu/blog/post/growth-mindset-vs-fixed-mindset

Creswell, J. D., & Khoury, B. (2019, October 30). Mindfulness meditation: A research-proven way to reduce stress. American Psychological Association. https://www.apa.org/topics/mindfulness/meditation#:~:text=Researchers%20reviewed%20more%20than%20200,%2C%20pain%2C%20smoking%20and%20addiction

D'Arcy, C. (2023). King Leonidas: Biography, facts & quotes. Study.com.

Dalaney, S. (2023, August 30). The distillation of Phil Jackson: A Zen master's approach to coaching & leadership. What Got You There. https://whatgotyouthere.com/the-distillation-of-phil-jackson-a-zen-masters-approach-to-coaching-leadership/

Davis, T. (2019, April 15). 15 ways to build a growth mindset. Psychology Today. https://www.psychologytoday.com/us/blog/click-here-for-happiness/201904/15-ways-to-build-a-growth-mindset

DeArdo, B. (2024, July 2). Tom Brady reveals one of his biggest regrets from his legendary NFL career: 'What the hell happened to me?' CBS Sports. https://www.cbssports.com/nfl/news/tom-brady-reveals-one-of-his-biggest-regrets-from-his-legendary-nfl-career-what-the-hell-happened-to-me/

Demetri, M. (n.d.). Michael Jordan mentality. Basketball Mindset Training. https://www.basketballmindsettraining.com/blog/michael-jordan-mentality

D'Heurle, A., & Feimer, J. N. (1975). A new image of the psyche: The archetypal psychology of James Hillman. University of North Carolina Press, 25(3), 289-298.

Ducksters. (n.d.). Tom Brady. https://www.ducksters.com/sports/tom_brady.php

Duckworth, A. (2016). Grit: The power of passion and perseverance. Scribner.

Etienne, V. (2023, November 28). Serena Williams says 'I am not ok today' in vulnerable social media post. People. https://people.com/serena-williams-says-i-am-not-ok-today-in-vulnerable-social-media-post-8407638

Finn, A. (2017, March 3). Scott Jurek: 'Being uncomfortable brings us back to our roots'. The Guardian. https://www.theguardian.com/lifeandstyle/the-running-blog/2017/mar/03/scott-jurek-being-uncomfortable-brings-us-back-to-our-roots

Football History. (n.d.). Pelé: The greatest footballer of all time. Retrieved July 10, 2024, from https://www.footballhistory.org/player/pele.html

Ford, B. D. (2018, April 22). Boston Marathon champ Desiree Linden: 'This is gonna be miserable'. ESPN. https://www.espn.com/olympics/story/_/id/23288605/as-desiree-linden-started-boston-marathon-knew-was-gonna-miserable-persevered-won

Gallo, C. (2019, August 30). Serena Williams gives a 3-step tutorial on mental toughness—Her greatest strength. Forbes. https://www.forbes.com/sites/carminegallo/2019/08/30/serena-williams-gives-a-3-step-tutorial-on-mental-toughness-her-greatest-strength/

Gupta, S. (2024, February 15). How self-compassion is linked to growth mindset. Learning While Human. https://learningwhilehuman.com/blog/how-self-compassion-is-linked-to-growth-mindset

Hillman, J. (1996). The soul's code. Random House.
Holstee. (n.d.). Personal, permanent, pervasive. Holstee. https://www.holstee.com/blogs/mindful-matter/personal-permanent-pervasive

Inc. (n.d.). 50 inspiring motivational quotes about willpower and determination. https://www.inc.com/jeff-haden/50-inspiring-motivational-quotes-about-willpower-and-determination.html

Irving, H. (2014, June 27). Keep calm and carry on – The compromise behind the slogan. History of Government Blog. https://history.blog.gov.uk/2014/06/27/keep-calm-and-carry-on-the-compromise-behind-the-slogan/

James, W. (n.d.). Quote. BrainyQuote. https://www.brainyquote.com/quotes/william_james_104186

Jelinek, J. (2022, January 11). Candle meditation: Can gazing at a flame increase your focus? Healthline. https://www.healthline.com/health/candle-meditation

Keflezighi, M. (2023, March 17). Meb Keflezighi: Take this time to start working on your weaknesses. Running for Real. https://runningforreal.com/meb-keflezighi/

Keng, S.-L., Smoski, M. J., & Robbins, C. J. (2013). Effects of mindfulness on psychological health: A review of empirical studies. Clinical Psychology Review, 33(6), 645-658. https://www.ncbi.nlm.nih.gov/pmc/articles/PMC3679190/

Kim, J., Kwon, J. H., Kim, J., Kim, E. J., Kim, H. E., Kyeong, S., & Kim, J.-J. (2021). The effects of positive or negative self-talk on the alteration of brain functional connectivity by performing cognitive tasks. Scientific Reports, 11(1). https://www.ncbi.nlm.nih.gov/pmc/articles/PMC8295361/

King, L. A. (2001). The health benefits of writing about life goals. Personality and Social Psychology Bulletin, 27(7), 798-807. https://doi.org/10.1177/0146167201277003

Kipchoge, E. (2019, May 30). Eliud's diaries - The collection. INEOS 1:59 Challenge. https://www.ineos159challenge.com/news/eliuds-diaries-the-collection

Lieberman, C. (2018, May 22). Why you should stop being so hard on yourself. The New York Times. https://www.nytimes.com/2018/05/22/smarter-living/why-you-should-stop-being-so-hard-on-yourself.html

Lines.com. (n.d.). Tom Brady. https://www.lines.com/nfl/players/tom-brady-4314

Mandella, N. (n.d.). Quote. Reflect & Respond. https://reflectandrespond.com/do-not-judge-me-by-my-success-nelson-mandela/

Mayer, B. A. (2022, January 11). Candle meditation: Can gazing at a flame increase your focus? Healthline. https://www.healthline.com/health/candle-meditation

McLeod, S. (2024, January 24). Maslow's hierarchy of needs. Simply Psychology. https://www.simplypsychology.org/maslow.html

Meacham, J. (2018, May/June). Winston Churchill: Portrait of power. Cigar Aficionado. https://www.cigaraficionado.com/article/winston-churchill-portrait-of-power

Mikkelsen, S. (2023, June 5). Michael Phelps: The training regimen of the most decorated swimmer in Olympic history. Olympics.com. https://olympics.com/en/news/michael-phelps-training-regimen-workut-diet

Morin, A. (2020, February 25). 10 exercises to make you mentally stronger. Psychology Today. https://www.psychologytoday.com/us/blog/what-mentally-strong-people-dont-do/202002/10-exercises-make-you-mentally-stronger

Mwangi, W. (2023, September 25). The legend Eliud Kipchoge. LinkedIn. https://www.linkedin.com/pulse/legend-eliud-kipchoge-william-mwangi-cipm/

National Center for Biotechnology Information. (n.d.). [Unspecified article]. https://www.ncbi.nlm.nih.gov/pmc/articles/PMC4152379/

Nelson, R. (2024). Pelé: The greatest footballer of all time. Football History. https://www.footballhistory.org/player/pele.html

Nicola, L. (2022, February 1). The Rafa mentality: How to perform under pressure. Neuroathletics. https://neuroathletics.substack.com/p/the-rafa-mentality-how-to-perform

Paffett, J. (2024, July 9). Neuroplasticity: The brain's ability to change and adapt to promote positive changes in mental health. Amputee Coalition. https://blog.amputee-coalition.org/education/neuroplasticity-the-brains-ability-to-change-and-adapt-to-promote-positive-changes-in-mental-health/

Performance Psychology Center. (n.d.). Performance psychology 101. https://www.performancepsychologycenter.com/post/performance-psychology-101

Perkins, N. (2023, October 16). The murder of Michael Jordan's father, explained. PopSugar. https://www.popsugar.com/celebrity/what-happened-to-michael-jordan-dad-49137020

Perry, E. (2022, October 11). 7 ways to overcome fear of failure and move forward in life. BetterUp. https://www.betterup.com/blog/how-to-overcome-fear-of-failure

Piccotti, T., & Biography.com Editors. (2023, August 9). Michael Jordan. Biography.com. https://www.biography.com/athletes/michael-jordan

Pryor, B. (2023, March 17). How Courtney Dauwalter keeps running simple. Trail Runner Magazine. https://www.trailrunnermag.com/training/how-courtney-dauwalter-keeps-her-running-fun/

Rational Badger. (2023, May 13). What can we learn from Roger Federer — the Swiss maestro. Medium. https://medium.com/@RationalBadger/what-can-we-learn-from-roger-federer-the-swiss-maestro-eca867155aa3

Raypole, C. (2019, February 25). How systematic desensitization can help you overcome fear. Healthline. https://www.healthline.com/health/systematic-desensitization

Reddy, S. (2023, October 4). David Beckham reflects on the 1998 World Cup red card and its aftermath. People. https://people.com/david-beckham-1998-world-cup-red-card-aftermath-8346982

Reid, S. (2023, July 9). Social support for stress relief. HelpGuide. https://www.helpguide.org/articles/stress/social-support-for-stress-relief.htm

Ronda, J. P. (1984). Lewis & Clark among the Indians: 9. The Way Home. University of Nebraska Press. https://lewisandclarkjournals.unl.edu/item/lc.sup.ronda.01.09

Roychowdhury, D. D. (2022). Using mental rehearsal to boost your performance and well-being in sport and exercise. Performance Psychology. https://www.drdevroy.com/mental-rehearsal-in-sport-and-exercise/#:~:text=That%20is%2C%20when%20engaging%20in,%2C%20or%20positive%20self%2Dtalk.

Sangerma, E. (2023, January 13). 7 traits of people with high emotional intelligence and 3 of their vices. Wholistique. https://medium.com/wholistique/7-traits-of-people-with-high-emotional-intelligence-5a5285b5785f

Schlossberg, M. (2016, June 4). These 22 quotes show why Muhammad Ali became the world's most famous athlete. Business Insider. https://www.businessinsider.com/muhammed-alis-most-famous-quotes-and-pre-fight-rhymes-2016-6

Schuman-Olivier, Z. (2020, November 6). Mindfulness and behavior change. National Center for Biotechnology Information. https://www.ncbi.nlm.nih.gov/pmc/articles/PMC7647439/

Scott, E. (2023, November 22). The toxic effects of negative self-talk. Verywell Mind. https://www.verywellmind.com/negative-self-talk-and-how-it-affects-us-4161304

Scullard, H. H. (2024, June 28). Scipio Africanus. Encyclopædia Britannica. https://www.britannica.com/biography/Scipio-Africanus

Seligman, M. E. P. (2006). Learned optimism: How to change your mind and your life. Vintage.

Seriously Science. (2014, November 13). Why is sitting by a fire so relaxing? Evolution may hold the key. Discover Magazine. https://www.discovermagazine.com/mind/why-is-sitting-by-a-fire-so-relaxing-evolution-may-hold-the-key

Singh, A. (2020, June 24). Types of self-talk (motivational & instructional self-talk). LinkedIn. https://www.linkedin.com/pulse/8-type-self-talk-motivational-instructional-arti-singh/

Smookler, E. (2023, June 30). The power of positive affirmations. Mindful. https://www.mindful.org/beginners-body-scan-meditation/

Sportco. (n.d.). The psychology of peak performance in sports. https://www.sportco.io/article/the-psychology-of-peak-performance-in-sports-584254

Srivastava, S., Tamir, M., McGonigal, K. M., John, O. P., & Gross, J. J. (2009, April). The social costs of emotional suppression: A prospective study of the transition to college. National Center for Biotechnology Information. https://www.ncbi.nlm.nih.gov/pmc/articles/PMC4141473/

Stanford Encyclopedia of Philosophy. (2022, December 7). Thomas Aquinas. Stanford Encyclopedia of Philosophy. https://plato.stanford.edu/entries/aquinas/

Steenbarger, B. (2018, February 17). Tapping the power of mental rehearsal. Forbes. https://www.forbes.com/sites/brettsteenbarger/2018/02/17/tapping-the-power-of-mental-rehearsal/

Sultana, N. (2024, June 7). Why am I underperforming in my sport? LinkedIn. https://www.linkedin.com/pulse/why-am-i-underperforming-my-sport-nicole-sultana-3aocc/

Teach Different. (n.d.). Do not judge me by my successes. Judge me by how many times I fell down and got back up again. https://teachdifferent.com/podcast/do-not-judge-me-by-my-successes-judge-me-by-how-many-times-i-fell-down-and-got-back-up-again-teach-different-with-nelson-mandela-resiliency/

Uhrig, A. (2020, September 8). The power of positive (and negative) affirmations. The Healing Tree. https://www.thehealingtreecc.org/blog/positive-affirmations

USA Basketball. (2015, November). How Michael Jordan's mindset made him a great competitor. https://www.usab.com/news/2015/11/how-michael-jordans-mindset-made-him-a-great-competitor

Very Big Brain. (2023, June 3). Effects of fire gazing on brain activity and relaxation. Very Big Brain. https://verybigbrain.com/outside-influences/effects-of-fire-gazing-on-brain-activity-and-relaxation/

Warrell, M. (2017, December 9). How to beat self-doubt and stop selling yourself short. Forbes. https://www.forbes.com/sites/margiewarrell/2017/12/09/doubt-your-doubts/

Webb Wright, K. (2023, March 9). The power of a mood journal: How writing can help manage emotions. Day One. https://dayoneapp.com/blog/mood-journal/

Wenger, S. (2022, January 25). Tom Brady feels 'gratitude' despite season-ending playoff loss and retirement talk. People. https://people.com/sports/tom-brady-feels-gratitude-despite-season-ending-playoff-loss-and-retirement-talk/

Williams, B. (2021, June 11). Michael Jordan's infamous NBA Finals 'Flu Game'. ESPN. https://www.espn.com/nba/story/_/id/31606593/the-truth-michael-jordan-infamous-nba-finals-flu-game

Wilson, M. (2020, July 24). The need to succeed: How fear of failure roadblocks our success. LinkedIn. https://www.linkedin.com/pulse/need-succeed-how-fear-failure-roadblocks-our-success-marya-wilson/

Wilson, P. A. (2015, August 31). Serena Williams is the best because of her brains – not just her body. The Guardian. https://www.theguardian.com/commentisfree/2015/aug/31/serena-williams-best-because-brains-not-body

Wong, A. (2023, May 30). Self-talk: How to change your inner voice. Psychology Today. https://www.psychologytoday.com/us/basics/self-talk

Wynn, T. (2012, December). Fire good. Make human inspiration happen. Smithsonian Magazine. https://www.smithsonianmag.com/science-nature/fire-good-make-human-inspiration-happen-132494650/

Yee, D. (2023). The effects of social comparison orientation on psychological well-being in social networking sites: Serial mediation of perceived social support and self-esteem. Journal of Media Psychology, 27(2), 119-133. https://www.ncbi.nlm.nih.gov/pmc/articles/PMC7556555/

Zhu, J. (2023, August 29). The fear of success: Understanding and overcoming the barriers to self-actualization. BetterMe. https://www.betterme.world/articles/the-fear-of-success/

www.ingramcontent.com/pod-product-compliance
Lightning Source LLC
Chambersburg PA
CBHW050244170426
43202CB00015B/2909